The Romans at Nostell P

Excavations at the new visitor car park in 2009

Dave Pinnock

with contributions by

Graham Bruce, Kay Hartley, Ruth Leary,
Gwladys Monteil, Mark Newman, Ellen Simmons
and Sophie Tibbles

Illustrations by

Berny McCluskey, Dave Pinnock
and Tim Robinson

On-Site Archaeology Monograph No.3
2013

A National Trust archaeological project

On-Site Archaeology Monograph No.3

Publisher
On-Site Archaeology Ltd.
25A Milton Street
York
YO10 3EP
Tel (01904) 411673
Fax (01904) 414522
http://www.onsitearchaeology.co.uk/

ISBN: 978-0-9561965-2-1

© National Trust 2013

General editors
Caroline Emery and Nick Pearson

Design and layout
Dave Pinnock

Printers
The Charlesworth Group
Flanshaw Way
Flanshaw Lane
Wakefield
WF2 9LP

Funded by
The National Trust
Registered charity no.205846

Front cover: Volunteers from South Leeds Archaeology, the Lifelong Learning Department at the University of Leeds and others; the main car park area from the air (photo: Martin Rowe); the stone-lined 'child's grave'.

Rear cover: Some members of the excavation team. James Stanley; Lauren McIntyre; Graham Bruce.

Contents

List of Figures

List of Plates

List of Tables

Acknowledgements

The project was designed and led by Mark Newman, National Trust Archaeological Consultant, who was also responsible for the overall project management in conjunction with Nick Pearson and Graham Bruce of On-Site Archaeology Ltd. Rebecca Remmer, Senior Archaeologist at the West Yorkshire Archaeology Advisory service, advised on the project design and her assistance added greatly to the value of the project. The archaeological fieldwork, excavation analysis and the publication of this volume were funded by the National Trust.

The excavations were directed by Graham Bruce and carried out by him, Caroline Emery, Sarah Everard, Berny McCluskey, Lauren McIntyre, Nick Pearson, Dave Pinnock, Tim Robinson, Alex Sotheran, James Stanley, and Alice Stone. Additional excavation was carried out by members of local archaeological societies as well as Mark Newman and other members of the National Trust team. The main excavation was carried out in the Autumn of 2009, in at times challenging weather conditions.

Various specialists contributed to the post-excavation analysis of the site: Ruth Leary, Kay Hartley and Gwladys Monteil (pottery), Ellen Simmons and Angela Walker (environmental evidence), Sophie Tibbles (CBM), Ian Panter and Kate Kenward (metal conservation), Cath Mortimer (industrial residues), Graham Bruce (glass), Dave Pinnock (querns) and Beta Analytic Inc (radiocarbon dating). The assessment report that formed the project design for this publication was written by Graham Bruce.

Final figures are by Dave Pinnock. The pottery was hand drawn by Tim Robinson and the querns by Berny McCluskey. Digitising of site drawings was by Katie Keefe and Berny McCluskey. This volume was proof read by Caroline Emery. The text was edited by Mark Newman and Dave Pinnock. Copy-editing, design and page layout were carried out by Dave Pinnock and the volume was printed by Charlesworth Group in Wakefield where the assistance of Lindsay Jennings and all the staff involved is gratefully acknowledged.

For their comments on and helpful suggestions regarding the contents of this volume, the author would like to thank Mark Newman; Graham Bruce, Caroline Emery and Nick Pearson (On-Site Archaeology Ltd); Ruth Leary; and Liz Humble (Senior Heritage Consultant at Purcell UK).

The book is intended to be of interest to both archaeological specialists and general readers. It is hoped that this tricky task has been achieved without failing either group.

Foreword

Mark Newman MA, MifA, FSA, Archaeological Consultant for the National Trust

There are moments that lift working in archaeology far beyond just being a job. The first is the frisson when the spade (literal or metaphorical) cuts the first edge of the first turf on a new site, its promise as yet unexplored. For me, that moment came at Nostell in 1997, when I opened my first trench there, adjacent to the mansion and – to everyone's surprise - encountered over six feet of stratified archaeological deposits.

Nostell was at that time all but a blank page archaeologically. Interest in the site had, not surprisingly, hitherto been dominated by the magnificent mansion and its contents. The vague recognition that there might be other archaeological resources on the site was little understood.

Since 1997, this situation has altered beyond any recognition. In progressive stages we have charted the vast archaeological resources relating to the setting of the mansion, in ancillary buildings such as the Stables, and in the outstanding designed landscapes that embrace it. Their development involved great Georgian architects and garden designers, whose confections were often modified by practical physical and financial limitations linked to rises and falls in the fortunes of the Winn family. Few of these fascinating stories, which constitute Nostell's unique tale, are recorded documentarily – they can only be unlocked through archaeological investigation.

Similarly, St. Oswald's Priory (which returned from obscurity to give the site its name in the early nineteenth century) has started to emerge. We can now map with confidence its location and form and have an outline understanding of the history of this nationally important – though puzzlingly little studied – monastic site. We have also started to understand the surrounding landscape on which the institution depended.

Also returning is the shadowy first Nostell Hall formed from the priory after the Dissolution. Almost completely forgotten, this was home to figures of national significance to Tudor England, and for a brief period would have been at the centre of the politics of northern England.

Just as the medieval priory's landscape formed the post-medieval, so too did earlier land use shape the landscape in which the priory itself was founded. There were both spiritual and practical roots to that foundation. Augustinian canons were not the zealots for harsh, basic, isolated, ascetic life that the Cistercians were. They were more firmly rooted in the secular world and established priories in places that articulated with this.

Initial opening up of the landscape probably owed most to the Iron Age/Romano-British period. This period was, in 1997, unknown at Nostell. It has become apparent since that the evidence is most certainly present across large tracts of the estate, if one is prompted to look for it.

One might think that Nostell has now told its stories, but that's very far from being the case. Only a proportion of the estate's archaeology has yet been found, and that has mainly been conserved safe and secure (but unexplored) in the ground. What is most remarkable about Nostell is that I have never encountered any rural site that has produced so many archaeological revelations, or, in places, such amazing depths of stratigraphy. In a landscape that succeeds brilliantly in appearing uncontrived, generations of labourers have, for different reasons, been enthusiastically levelling ridges and filling hollows. The result is a bonanza for archaeological conservation.

And the property has very far from finished giving up its secrets. Past the first thrill of starting work, and the obvious excitement of each day's discoveries on site, comes archaeology's next adventure – working out what it all means. Often this is a great deal more than one had realised while out on site, as is demonstrated in the pages of this book.

Our finds on the car park site go way beyond a first clear view of Romano-British presence on the property. Now we can see that this was another lost moment at which Nostell played a role on the regional if not national stage, as a cog in the mighty Roman military machine. Remains of that presence may even have invited in the first spiritual interest on the site nearly 1000 years later.

The project also left us with promises for the future. The archaeology reported here clearly extended well beyond the limits of the examined site, both physically and chronologically. Nostell's next archaeological frisson is knowing that the future undoubtedly holds new opportunities to explore it further.

Prologue

Graham Bruce of On-Site Archaeology Ltd. Director of the Nostell car park excavation

As a professional archaeologist employed predominantly by developers and builders on projects required as part of the planning process, most of my working life is geared around avoiding surprises. We do all in our power to try and predict what archaeology may be present on a site in advance, as the unexpected is what makes developers nervous. This professional attitude is somewhat at odds with the popular view of archaeological discovery and, indeed, the image of an archaeologist that inspires people to join the profession in the first place.

Like any other archaeological investigation carried out in advance of development, the project at the new visitor car park at Nostell Priory was planned in such a way as to minimize unexpected discoveries. Despite this, it still managed to produce surprising archaeological results at every stage.

Before excavation had started a detailed assessment of all known archaeological and historical information had been assembled. This suggested that this part of the Nostell estate was relatively undisturbed in the post medieval period when other parts of the estate were the subject of grand landscaping schemes. Before that landscaping, during the time of the medieval priory, it was most likely to have been farmland, away from the main monastic complex. Although some evidence for prehistoric and Romano-British agricultural land use was known from the surrounding area there was nothing to suggest that this was certainly going to be present on the site of the new car park.

The next stage of assessing the archaeological potential took the form of a geophysical survey, employing a suite of remote sensing techniques that allow us to 'see' beneath the soil by measuring variations in magnetic fields and electrical conductivity. The first surprise of the project was that this provided what initially appeared to be interesting results, including the remains of a possible prehistoric pit alignment and other intriguing anomalies. Full of anticipation, we opened a series of trial trenches in order to evaluate these possible features… which proved not to exist! The inclusions in the topsoil and variations in the underlying sandstone had conspired to give the appearance of archaeological features. However, the next surprise at this stage was that genuine archaeological features were present in the trenches that had not been detected by the geophysical survey. These included ditches, pits, postholes and a small quantity of pottery dated to the Romano-British period. The trial trenching had shown that the site was going to contain some archaeological remains, but at that point it was difficult to understand what the features meant. Were they evidence of a settlement or of field systems linked with a farmstead? Were the remains all from the Romano-British period or were we looking at overlying features from many different periods of history and prehistory?

The trial trenches revealed enough to prompt the redesign of the foundation of the car park to ensure that as little archaeology was disturbed as possible and to make sure that a full excavation was carried out in those areas where disturbance was unavoidable. Stripping off of the topsoil in preparation for the excavation showed that the site contained much more in the way of archaeological features than the trial trenches had made us think. They had been sited, by chance, in some of the less archaeologically rich areas of the site. Not only were there many more ditches and pits than the trial trenches indicated, but there were more complicated structures, including an oven, a corn-drier, clay-lined pits and possible burials. The relationships between a number of the features hinted that the site had been occupied over a prolonged period with changes to the layout taking place. The excavation went on to show that we were in what looked like a long-lived rural settlement or farmstead from the Romano-British period, even though this probably extended beyond the area that was available for investigation. Several apparently similar farmsteads of this date have been identified across this area of Yorkshire and the impression, as the excavation progressed, was that we had discovered another one.

A final revelation was still to come, though. When all of the finds had been cleaned and looked at by specialists, the pottery was found to be typical of a collection that you would only expect to find in a Roman town or a fort, and was totally unlike the normal assemblage for a rural farmstead of the period. As this book will show, the implications of this for our understanding of the site at Nostell were profound and a project like this certainly reminds us that it is the surprises that interest us in archaeological discovery in the first place.

Plate 1. Nostell Priory looking southwest
(photo: National Trust)

Part 1

Introduction and Site Background

1.1 Introduction

Nostell Priory is an impressive Palladian mansion, built in 1733 and set by a lake in extensive parkland. The house and grounds have been in the care of the National Trust since 1953, although Lord and Dowager Lady St Oswald (of the Winn family who owned Nostell for 300 years from 1654) retain strong links with the property. An internationally recognised architectural masterpiece, the mansion's majestic appearance attracts large numbers of visitors (Plate 1). They are drawn too by the splendid Robert Adams interiors, the Chippendale furniture and important oil paintings as well as the beautiful landscaped setting that extends to around 300 acres. This last was acquired by the National Trust, through a generous grant from the Heritage Lottery Fund, in 2004.

For many people the attraction of Nostell Priory is given a further dimension by the fact that the house and gardens were built on the site of a now vanished medieval monastery, an Augustinian priory founded in the early twelfth century and dedicated to St Oswald. No grand ruins comparable to Fountains or Rievaulx remain, yet historical sources show that, from its initial foundation to its demise, St Oswald's Priory was a rich and powerful institution. Like the other monasteries, it was surrendered to the Crown as part of the extraordinary events during the English Reformation that have come to be known as the Dissolution of the Monasteries, which so profoundly influenced the social and geographical landscape of the country. Surrendered in 1540, and immediately given to one of the Royal Commissioners who were responsible for valuing the monastic estates on behalf of Henry VIII, unfortunately little now remains above ground of the extensive priory complex. It would once have included the canons' church and cloistral buildings such as chapter house, dormitory, refectory (dining hall) and kitchens as well as buildings and features that served the more secular concerns of the large farming enterprise that serviced the priory, such as barns, stables, bakeries, mills, fishponds and paddocks.

Only three buildings survive from the monastic period at Nostell. The Church of St Michael and Our Lady was built in its present form shortly before the Dissolution and now stands slightly incongruously within the parkland of the estate. This was not the priory church but was built separately by the canons to serve the parish of Wragby, a function it still fulfils. Within the eighteenth century Nostell Home Farm complex, between the church and the stables, are two other monastic buildings, the so-called 'refectory' dating from 1509-10 and 'brewhouse' from 1481. Despite their later names both buildings probably served the monastic farmers as large barns for crop storage and processing (WYAS HBRS 1996, Wrathmell 2005). The former may indeed be the wool warehouse whose construction, in the early fifteenth century, is recorded in accounts of the priory (Brockwell 1915, Burton 1785, Mark Newman *pers comm*).

Such then, apart from occasional tantalising glimpses of buried medieval stonework uncovered by small-scale archaeological investigations near to the mansion (OSA 2008a), are the medieval remains at Nostell. Until the archaeological investigation described in this volume little was known of the development of the landscape before the founding of the priory, the date and circumstances of which themselves are – as the Victoria County History asserts – "not free from obscurity" (Page 1974, 231). Medieval documents suggest that there was a group of hermits living here before the priory was founded, as early as 1109 or even before, although nothing is really known of the nature of their community (NAA 2001, Frost 2007).

The archaeological investigation recorded here may not have done anything to illuminate the gloom of the Dark Ages, but it did reveal that the land now occupied by the Nostell estate was also inhabited by people at an even earlier date, during the Romano-British period (43 – 410 AD) and in the Iron Age. The discovery of significant Roman remains was a surprise. It has previously been suggested that the modern A638 running past the site lies on the course of a Roman road but this suggestion was not based on the discovery of any physical remains, just on projecting the course of sections

1

of road known elsewhere. Apart from that, the Romans have been relatively unknown in the vicinity of Nostell. The nearest major Roman settlements are at Doncaster and Castleford. Although there have been a number of stray finds of Roman coins and pottery found over the years at nearby Wakefield and Pontefract (and in the wider area) it is not thought that the Romans established a presence in these places; instead the finds are likely to represent the adoption of elements of Roman material culture by native peoples.

The discovery of the unexpected is of course the very essence of archaeology, and each new discovery adds to the cumulative sum of knowledge, joining with other jigsaw pieces to show an ever more complex picture of the past. It is also true that the harder one looks, the more interesting the picture often becomes. This was certainly true at Nostell where post excavation analysis of the already remarkable findings was to reveal a remarkable Roman military connection that may help to rewrite the history of the Roman conquest and occupation of the region. It also raises the intriguing possibility that the community of hermits who lived at Nostell before the founding of the priory in the early twelfth century, concerning whom very little is known, may have deliberately chosen to adopt a site with Roman associations. Although direct evidence has yet to be found of a link, it would be in keeping with early medieval Christian practice where the deliberate siting of churches and other religious institutions at former Roman centres is well attested.

1.2 The site and its setting

The site location and circumstances of the project

Nostell Priory lies to the north of the main A638 road from Wakefield to Doncaster close to the village of Wragby, approximately 8km southeast of the centre of Wakefield, in West Yorkshire. The area of the property that was the subject of this investigation is now the visitor car park and is situated close to the main entrance off the A638, a twentieth century modification to the estate's boundaries known as the Eagle Gates, adjacent to the Church of St Michael and Our Lady. The car park is approximately centred at National Grid Reference (NGR) SE 409 172 (Figure 1).

Archaeological investigation was prompted by the planned construction of this car park. Widening year-round public access to Nostell's parkland was central to the 2004 Heritage Lottery Fund grant, and this has obviously driven up visitor numbers. This increase demanded more parking space, which (combined with a desire to remove the need for cars to be driven in front of the mansion and be parked in full view of its main eastern elevation, as had been necessary with the old car park) led to plans for the construction of a new car park. The new build needed to fit unobtrusively within the eighteenth century landscape design but at a walkable distance for able-bodied visitors to the mansion. It also needed to be convenient for those just making use of the parkland walks. The position of the new visitor car park was the only possible choice, avoiding impact on the recognised designed landscape and the key views to and from the house itself.

Prior to the archaeological project taking place the site had formed part of a large area of pasture used for grazing cattle. Topographically the majority of the site lies on a broad ridge extending to the south and west from the mansion at approximately 60 metres above Ordnance Datum (AOD), although the adjoining land slopes down to approximately 43 metres AOD at Hardwick Beck, 600 metres to the north (see Figure 25). The underlying geology of the area consists of carboniferous coal measures. The coal measures are generally made up of grey mudstones and siltstones with subordinate fine-grained sandstones.

Previous archaeological and historical knowledge of the site

Before the findings of the present work, archaeological understanding of the site and its immediate surroundings was dominated by the medieval period and later. An archaeological survey, including analysis of historic maps, undertaken for the National Trust (NAA 2001) suggested that the priory church was located close to the kitchen pavilion at the southwest corner of the present-day mansion. Archaeological trenching, undertaken in 2008 to the north and south of the kitchen pavilion, revealed substantial foundations that are thought to have formed part of this church (OSA 2008a). This would place the site of the visitor car park considered by this report over 500m to the east of the main cloistral complex. However, the entire area of the present parkland (and considerable tracts of land beyond) lay within the priory's ownership, including the site of the new car park (Newman

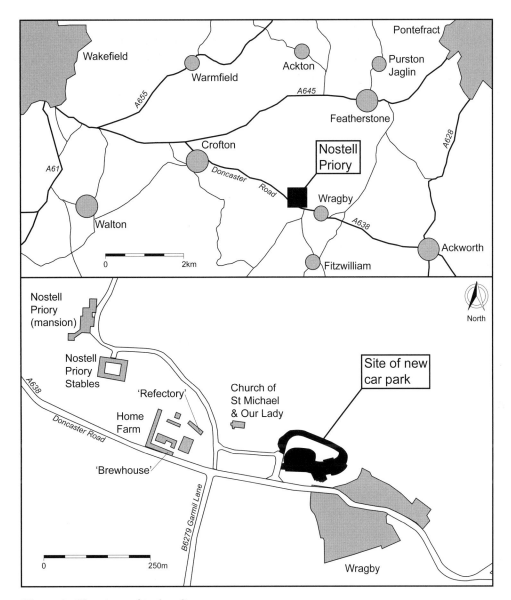

Figure 1. The site and its locality

2002). There was also an old tradition, recorded in the Nostell Priory Act Book dating from the 15th century, that the location of the original hermitical community was where the church of St Michael and our Lady stands and that the priory was moved to its later location when refounded under Prior Adelwald in the second decade of the twelfth century (NAA 2001, Frost 2007).

Immediately following the Dissolution, the church, chancel and chapter house were demolished with the remaining buildings converted to a mansion for Thomas Leigh, a Royal Commissioner. A deer park was established during the late sixteenth or early seventeenth century and by the middle of the seventeenth century the property had passed into the hands of the Winn family. Major changes occurred after 1730 when the fourth Baronet started work on the creation of the present house, a project that ran for many decades and involved the eventual demo-

lition of the old house around 1780. It was during the course of this evolution that the present-day designed landscape was laid out, involving Robert Adam in the 1760s and 1770s. However, all available map evidence from the eighteenth century onwards suggested that the area of the estate within which the new car park lies was broadly unaffected by these changes and remained as undeveloped parkland grazing or agricultural pasture throughout the post-medieval and into the modern period.

Although the archaeological potential of this site was predominantly understood to relate to the known medieval and later use, there were also some slight indications of earlier archaeological features elsewhere. Cropmarks visible on aerial photographs of the surrounding area suggested that field systems (and possibly settlements) of late prehistoric and Romano-British date might be present. Cropmarks are formed when plants grow above archaeological features that, although no longer visible on the surface, can lead to either accelerated or retarded growth compared with the crop growing on adjoining ground. Such marks had been identified to the northeast of the stable block at Nostell, approximately 400 metres to the northwest of the proposed new car park, as well as at several other places in the wider vicinity (NAA 2001, OSA 2008b). These small-scale systems of small rectangular fields are often associated with enclosures and roundhouses forming farming settlements and are common to both the Romano-British period and the preceding later Iron Age. One of these farming settlements shown up by cropmarks has been excavated at South Elmsall, about 6 miles southeast of Nostell, and was found to span both periods (Ottaway 2003, Chadwick 2009). Part of a very similar settlement of Romano-British date was excavated at Apple Tree Close, Pontefract (Turner 1987).

A small archaeological excavation beneath the so-called Refectory building in March 2008 (located less than 200 metres to the west of the site of the proposed car park) revealed two large ditches, one of which contained Romano-British pottery (OSA 2008c). This suggested that the field system seen on aerial photographs northeast of the stables might have been more extensive than was apparent from the air, a point reiterated by the discovery of several ditches and pits excavated near the original crop-

marks. These were found in a long north-south aligned trench that was excavated across the main east vista in front of (i.e. just to the west of) the mansion to open the route for a new sewer, in the summer of 2008 (OSA 2008a). Although only a very small amount of putative Roman pottery was found, the snapshot of archaeological features offered by the trench was consistent with a field system and potentially settlement-related pits of probable Iron Age or Romano-British date.

The A638 road, forming the southern boundary of the site, may follow the course of a Roman road as has been proposed in records held by the West Yorkshire Historic Environment Record archive (HER references PRN 3499-3502). This was just based upon projecting the line of a road that is known to have run from Elslack (*Olenacum*) Roman fort near Skipton, through Keighley, to Bradford (Margary 1973, road 721; NAA 2001) rather than the discovery of any physical remains. Neither Ivan Margary nor the West Yorkshire Archaeological Survey (Faull and Moorhouse 1981) included the road on their maps. That said, the projected line of the road would run near the remains of a temporary Roman military camp discovered more recently at Kirkhamgate (Esmonde Cleary 1997, Ottaway 2003), a mile northwest of Wakefield, which lends some further credibility to the suggestion (Figure 2).

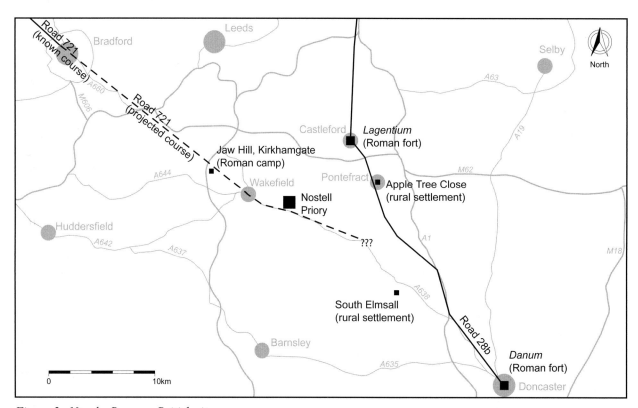

Figure 2. Nearby Romano-British sites

The closest major Roman sites to Nostell are the fort of *Lagentium* at Castleford and the fort of *Danum* at Doncaster. The A639, which formed the main Roman road between Doncaster and Castleford, runs 6km east and northeast of Nostell (Margary 1973, road 28b).

1.3 Evaluation and excavation methods

Evaluating the archaeological potential of the site

In the spring and summer of 2008, as part of the planning for the new visitor car park, the proposed site was archaeologically evaluated. The purpose of the evaluation was to establish the extent and assess the significance of any archaeological remains that might have been present beneath the turf and topsoil, and to work out an appropriate strategy for either minimizing the damage to any surviving remains or recording them if damage was unavoidable.

An initial geophysical survey using the techniques of resistivity and magnetometry was carried out at the site (Gaffney 2008). It identified several anomalies potentially of archaeological origin in the area of the proposed new car park including possible pits and ditches of unknown date. As a result of these findings four evaluation trenches were excavated by On-Site Archaeology Ltd, one measuring 15 metres by 10 metres and the others 10 metres by 5 metres (OSA 2008d). The trenches were initially opened using a JCB mechanical excavator fitted with a toothless bucket, undertaken under close archaeological supervision down to the first significant archaeological horizon. Where archaeological features were encountered cut into undisturbed natural geology, a sample of sufficient size was investigated to determine the archaeological character of the features and the remainder left *in-situ*.

The evaluation confirmed the archaeological potential of the site revealing evidence of Romano-British settlement. Archaeological features were identified in three of the four trenches excavated, consisting of ditches, pits and occasional postholes, several of which contained small fragments of Romano-British pottery. Interestingly, the features discovered during the evaluation did not correspond with the anomalies shown in the geophysical survey, but anomalous results in geophysical surveys are not uncommon and can be heavily influenced by the local geology and topsoil contamination. Indeed, sandstone bedrock as found at Nostell is known to frequently provide poor responses in geophysical surveys (English Heritage 2008).

The excavation methodology

Despite the archaeological discoveries no alternative site could be found for the car park that met the site's requirements, especially the importance of respecting the eighteenth century designed landscape, and the need to serve visitors to the park. Instead, the proposed construction methods were modified to minimise impact on buried remains and a specification for a large-scale archaeological excavation was developed by the National Trust with On-Site Archaeology Ltd and agreed following consultation with the West Yorkshire Archaeological Advisory Service. The objective of the excavation was to examine, record and interpret any archaeological remains disturbed by the development, initially to be achieved through archaeological excavation in areas of the site considered to have the highest potential, with scope to expand into other (initially sampled) peripheral areas if deemed necessary. Due to inconsistent preservation of the anticipated archaeology and the varying degree of impact of groundworks in different zones of the development, the precise nature of archaeological investigation varied across the site (Figure 3).

In Autumn 2009 open-area excavation was undertaken in the western areas of the main car park (Plate 2) and access road where the impact of the development, and the potential for archaeology indentified by the evaluation, were at their greatest. This consisted of careful topsoil stripping by mechanical excavator down to the level at which the archaeological features cut the natural sandstone geology, followed by hand excavation of the archaeological features. An unexcavated 'island' was left in the centre of the car park area to protect the roots of a mature tree. As will be seen below, the excavation revealed the presence of a complex archaeological site within these areas of the development site.

In the eastern areas of the main car park and the access road, the anticipated archaeological potential and the impact of the proposed ground works were less significant than in the west. Following mechanical excavation of upper topsoil from the

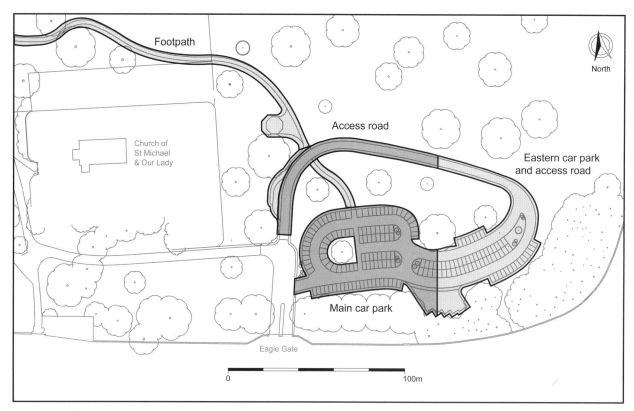

Figure 3. The site layout
(dark grey=full excavation, light grey=watching brief/evaluation trenching only)

Plate 2. The main car park under excavation, looking east

whole area, six north-south aligned trenches each measuring two metres wide and covering a combined linear distance of approximately 225 metres were then machine excavated through to the surface of the natural sandstone. Potential archaeological features exposed were then hand excavated but most of these 'features' proved to be natural variations in the bedrock or resulted from tree root disturbance. Due to the absence of archaeologically significant features within these trenches, and the shallow depth of proposed groundworks, no further archaeological investigation (or further ground disturbance) was undertaken within the eastern area of the car park.

In addition to the archaeological investigation undertaken for the construction of the car park surface and access road, several small trenches were excavated to a depth of 600mm below the modern ground surface for proposed soakaways adjacent to the edge of the main excavated areas, . In addition, various smaller works associated with the project were examined by archaeological watching brief, but these are reported on elsewhere (OSA 2009).

The excavation team comprised eleven professional archaeologists. As with most archaeological work carried out by On-Site Archaeology Ltd, the overall structure of the team was organized with little hierarchy, using experienced excavation staff who each took responsibility for understanding the overall site context of their work (as discussed in Fenton-Thomas 2011). Although key decisions were made by the site director there were no formal supervisors. A small number of less experienced archaeologists also worked alongside the more experienced members and developed their professional skills in the process. In addition a number of members of local community archaeology groups (South Leeds Archaeology and the Lifelong Learning Department at the University of Leeds) and National Trust staff assisted in the excavation during the course of two weekend sessions towards the end of the main excavation. Community participation of this sort is a valuable, albeit sadly uncommon, addition to an archaeological investigation, bringing a range of experience and new perspectives as well as allowing more intensive examination of the site than might otherwise be possible. The professional excavation examined the sample of excavated features required to meet planning conditions; the volunteer archaeologists usefully extended this sample – a particular benefit given the unusual and important nature of the artefactual assemblage recovered.

Part 2

The Excavation Results

2.1 Report structure and the phasing of the site

This report consists of an account of the excavation results, description of the artefacts recovered and a discussion of the integrated findings. It is focused on the Iron Age and Roman period features found during the excavation of the western part of the new visitor car park and its access road, referred to throughout this volume as the 'main car park' and 'access road'. Although features from the early modern period were found in these areas, they were few in number and have been reported on elsewhere (OSA 2009). Neither does this report consider other parts of the development that were investigated in which no Iron Age or Romano-British archaeological remains were found, such as the eastern part of the car park, the footpath linking the car park to the existing infrastructure of the property, a staff and disabled car park and its access track and various smaller works to accommodate services. In these areas early modern features relating to the history of the estate from the eighteenth century onward were found. The excavation on the line of the main link footpath encountered a pair of parallel clay banks and an adjacent ditch, all orientated north-south and dating from between the eleventh and the fourteenth centuries, just to the north and northwest of Wragby parish church. These too are reported on elsewhere (OSA 2009).

The excavation revealed the presence of a complex site in which five main phases of activity have been identified, ranging in date from the pre-Roman Iron Age to the mid fourth century AD (Table 1). The chronological phasing of the site is based primarily upon the assessment of recovered pottery assemblages, enhanced where possible by analysis of stratigraphic relationships and the orientation and spatial correspondence between dated and undated features. There are occasions, particularly with regard to the earliest and latest phases, when a lack of precision in the dating of the pottery assemblages means that there may be a degree of temporal overlap between the phases. This is noted in the text.

Discussion of the site naturally falls into phases but as with any analytical division of this sort it is, to varying degrees, an artificial construct. Such is demanded by both the limited nature of the archaeological record and the necessity of structuring the description and discussion of the site in a logical manner. It is important to note therefore that the phases should not be taken to necessarily imply a discontinuity between the activity of one phase and the next. Sometimes this is so, as is the case with the transition from phase 2 to phase 3 but, for example, there is evidence to suggest an element of continuity of landscape division from the pre-Roman Iron Age phase into the early Roman while the well in the centre of the main car park may have been in use throughout the entire Romano-British period.

Phase	Description
Phase1	Pre-Roman Iron Age, roughly pre-70 AD (in the north of England)
Phase 2	Early Roman, characterised by pottery from the Flavian-Trajanic period (69-117 AD)
Phase 3	Mid to late second century
Phase 4	Third century
Phase 5	Late third – fourth century

Table 1. Site phasing

Because of the absence of datable artefacts or stratigraphic relationships in a substantial proportion of the features, it has not been possible to place all of the excavated archaeology securely within the phases outlined below. There are also uncertainties regarding the identification of some of the pottery assemblages given close similarities between some pottery fabrics assigned to the pre-Roman Iron Age and those of the first and second centuries AD, making secure attribution to phases difficult. In addition to the dating provided by the pottery assemblage one of the features, which did not contain period-specific artefacts, was assigned to phase by radiocarbon dating of charcoal in its fill.

Throughout the report dates are expressed in terms of 'phases', centuries, and sometimes as periods defined by Roman imperial dynasties such as Flavian, Trajanic, etc., a common practice among specialists in the Romano-British period. Although the actual dates of these periods are included in parentheses for the convenience of readers, the use of the dynastic references is intended to convey "less clear cut implications of exactitude" than the use of calendar dates (Webster 1976, 5).

For readers unfamiliar with archaeological reports it is worth noting that the standard method of archaeological recording as used in this volume is to assign every discrete unit of excavated ground or cut feature revealed (both known as a 'context') a unique identifier or 'context number'. This applies to both material that has been deposited on the ground surface or in a feature (identified by a number in round brackets) and to the interface or 'cut' left when material has been excavated in the past (in which case the context numbers are shown in square brackets). Thus a simple pit may have been dug into the bedrock. This pit would be assigned a context number in square brackets, say [100]. Perhaps it was slowly part-filled by the products of natural erosion – which would be given a context number in round brackets, for example (99) - and then at a later date deliberately filled with more soil to level the ground, also assigned a separate number e.g. (98). In this way, we would describe the feature as a pit [100] with two fills (99) and (98). Among other advantages to this system, it allows for the unique identification of every feature

on the site and the accurate location of every artefact recovered.

2.2 Results

Phase 1: Pre-Roman Iron Age

This earliest phase of activity is represented by a small number of features containing pottery of this date within their fills (Figure 4). A relatively small number of sherds (23) were recovered. However, the dating of handmade pottery in this region is imprecise and it is recognised that ceramics of this type continued in use, especially on rural sites, beyond the Roman conquest, and even into the early second century AD (Leary, this volume). It is therefore possible that there may be a degree of overlap between this phase and the next (early Roman) phase. On the other hand, as Leary comments of some of the handmade pottery, "it is very unlikely that these pots were used by the same people who used the fully Romanised vessels of Flavian-Trajanic type and these are more likely to represent pre-Flavian [i.e. pre-69 AD] activity on the site", although she acknowledges that the cruder handmade pots may have been traded at the later date for their contents. The remains from this period thus may represent evidence for the land divisions and other features of the pre-Roman landscape or they may be a part and parcel of the same landscape that developed in phase 2. That several of the features assigned to this phase contained only a single sherd of datable pottery is also a reason for caution. The only feature that seems certain to be pre-Roman in date is the relatively massive but enigmatic north-south orientated ditch [1220].

Postholes and small pits

The discrete features whose fills contained phase 1 pottery consisted of five pits/large postholes within the main car park: [1492] which contained 2 sherds in its fill; [1464] with 7 sherds, and [1648] which had one sherd; and postholes [1446] and [1405] (with 5 and 4 sherds respectively). Also included is a single posthole with a stone post pad setting for a substantial timber post in the base [1282] in the access road (Plate 3), which contained 17 handmade sherds from a single vessel of pre-Roman Iron Age date or later. The pits and postholes

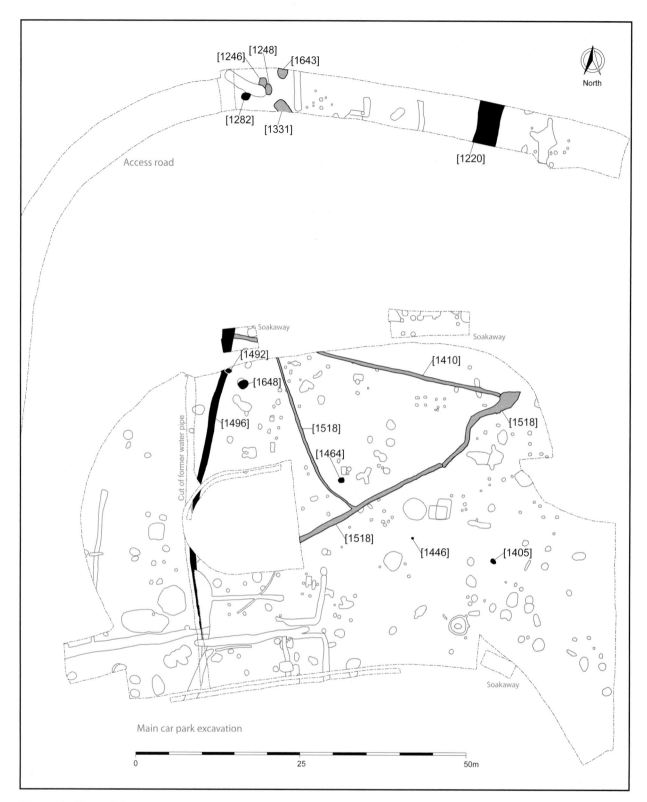

Figure 4. Phase 1 features
(Black = securely dated, grey = poorly dated)

found containing pottery dating to this phase are widely scattered but, with the exception of [1282], they appear to form an irregular southeast-north-west alignment within the car park area, suggest-ing they may derive from a possible boundary in a similar way to the ditches described below. Within

2.5 metres of post setting [1282] were two shallow oval pits [1246] and [1248]. These were 1.2 metres and 0.9 metres in diameter, and each contained a single fill of yellow brown silty sand, contain-ing frequent natural sandstone fragments and rare flecks of charcoal, but no finds. Their proximity to

Plate 3. Phase 2 ditch [1279] cutting through post setting [1282]

[1282] and the fact that all three features were cut by the same phase 2 feature (ditch [1279]) suggests that they may date to this earlier phase. Another similar shallow undated pit [1643] was revealed during the extension of the trench to the north for the construction of a soakaway.

Linear boundaries

Ironically, given the relative lack of artefacts within it, the feature most certain to date to this phase is the deep, wide ditch [1220]. The original cut of the ditch [1220] (Plate 4 and Figure 6) was of considerable size being 3.5 metres wide and 2.1 metres deep (measured at the edge of the trench from the top of the modern topsoil), making it by far the biggest ditch on the site but only – frustratingly – revealed in the narrow confines of the access road. No continuation or return was observed in any other part of the site. It contained three gradually accumulated fills, in the uppermost of which was a single

11

Plate 4. Ditch [1220] looking north

sherd of indeterminate pottery of possible Iron Age date. While the evidence of one poorly dated sherd alone is not definitive enough to place this feature confidently into phase 1 on its own, the gradual accumulation of the silty fills combined with the fact that a relatively shallow re-cut [1251] containing a massive assemblage of early Romano-British pottery followed the top of the ditch, is supportive of a phase 1 date. It is highly unlikely that the three fills of the ditch, with their slowly-accumulated appearance, would have had time to be laid down in the early Roman phase before the re-cut was dug and then backfilled with its well-dated pottery assemblage.

The terminus of a steep-sided northwest-southeast ditch [1331], measuring 1.5 metres wide and 0.7 metres deep, contained a single sherd of handmade pottery in its uppermost fill though it did not have a stratigraphic relationship with any other features. Its secondary fill appeared to be a deliberate backfill, covering the primary fill that may have been made up of the remains of a bank that originally stood next to the ditch. Although any interpretation based on a single sherd is tentative, especially as the sherd was very abraded which suggests that it may have been residual (i.e. redeposited at least once from its original context and therefore older than the context in which it was found), this ditch may have been backfilled before the Romano-British period. However, as is noted below, the juxtaposition of a section of nearby ditch containing early Romano-British pottery hints that [1331] may belong in fact to the early Romano-British phase.

An approximately northeast-southwest aligned ditch [1496] (Plate 5) towards the western side of the main car park area was cut by and therefore pre-dated pit/large posthole [1492] which contained 2 sherds of pottery of possible pre-Roman date. The ditch did not contain any dating evidence itself but must be earlier than the pit/posthole.

A narrow, approximately east-west aligned, linear [1410] at the northern part of the main car park area may also belong to this earliest phase of activity. It was cut by a later linear pit [1502] containing phase 2 pottery in its fill. Its early dating is suggested by the fact that it is approximately perpendicular to [1496] and appeared to therefore be contemporary with it. A poorly defined, undated, network of linear features [1518], interpreted as possible hedge-lines, that ran northeast-southwest and northwest-southeast across the central part of the main car park excavation area, seems to have been respected by the orientation of [1410] in a way that suggests that they were contemporary. If so, this would have – with [1410] and [1496] - created two triangular enclosures.

Plate 5. Ditch [1496] looking south

Phase 2: Early Roman (late first to early second century AD)

The ceramic evidence (Leary, Hartley and Monteil, this volume) has dated the fills of several features within the main car park area and access road to the Flavian-Trajanic (69-117 AD) period, which sees Roman expansion into the north of England and the construction of a number of forts to consolidate occupation in the early 70s. The remains that are datable to this phase are characterised by the presence of an unusual assemblage of pottery types associated solely with Roman military sites. There is evidence for land divisions, for water management in the form of a probable well and clay-lined lined cisterns, and for an oven (Figure 5).

Land divisions

In the access road, a broad, relatively shallow re-cut [1251] of the substantial earlier ditch [1220] contained a significant assemblage of pottery (896 sherds, concentrated in the primary fill of the recut) dated to the late first century. The pottery's forms parallel those found in the first phase of Castleford fort, and were found along with a large number of pieces of daub and a fragment of Roman brick or tile. The original cut of the ditch was 2.1 metres deep (measured at the trench edge from the top of modern day topsoil) and 3.5 metres wide, but the re-cut, while the same width was only 1.25 metres deep. Assuming that the ditch was of pre-Roman date, as seems likely, redefinition of its alignment suggests that elements of the earlier landscape were still visible in phase 2 and continued in use, albeit in a modified form. As with the original ditch, there was no continuation visible elsewhere on the site.

Shallow linear pit [1502], which was 3 metres long, up to 1.5 metres wide and only 0.1 metres deep, had five late first to early second century pottery sherds in its single fill. While no continuation was seen, it is possible that this shallow feature is the only surviving part of a longer shallow ditch, but this is speculation explaining an otherwise enigmatic feature.

A northwest-southeast aligned, steep-sided elongated pit [1279] had a single fill, which contained 5 scraps of early Romano-British greyware. The feature had a total length of 6.9 metres, was 1.6 metres wide, with steep sides and flat base at a

depth of 0.48 metres. It appears to have been a short section of ditch and was on roughly the same alignment as the possible Iron Age ditch [1331], from the termination of which this was separated by about 2 metres. It is tempting to see this separation as an entrance and to deduce that both ditches were contemporary and belong to this early Romano-British phase, despite the differing nature of the pottery present in their backfills.

A possible ditch terminus [1623] at the northern limits of the excavation provided additional evidence of land division in this area during this phase as it contained 14 sherds of late first to early second century pottery in its fill. The feature was 0.4 metres deep and 1.1 metres wide but only lay within the access road excavation by a length of 0.6 metres, so reliable interpretation was impossible; it could also have been a steep-sided, deep pit.

Three ditches [1010/1018/1024/1055/1057], [1201] and [1203/1383], dated by pottery to this phase, were recorded in the southwest corner of the main car park area. North-south ditch [1201] had been heavily truncated by several later ditches and a trench for a modern water pipe, making its interpretation difficult. The ditch was a maximum of 2.5 metres wide, with gently sloping sides running to a flat base at a maximum depth of 0.3 metres. At its northern edge it appeared to truncate the remains of phase 1 ditch [1496], which continued to the north, so it may have been a reiteration of the boundary from the earlier phase indicating that [1496] was still visible despite having been backfilled and may have remained in use into this early Romano-British phase. Ditch [1201] contained a single fill in which a small quantity of late first to early second century pottery was found.

The more northern of the two east-west ditches was [1203/1383]. At its west end this was relatively insubstantial, at only 0.45 metres wide and 0.15 metres deep, but it increased in size towards the east, to 1.2 metres wide and 0.45 metres deep at its terminus, 10.5 metres from ditch [1201]. This ditch appears to have been contemporary with [1201]. Only a single fill was present in the shallower part, which contained mid to late first to early second century pottery including the earliest fragment of samian ware recovered from the site. In the terminus a relatively thick primary erosion fill

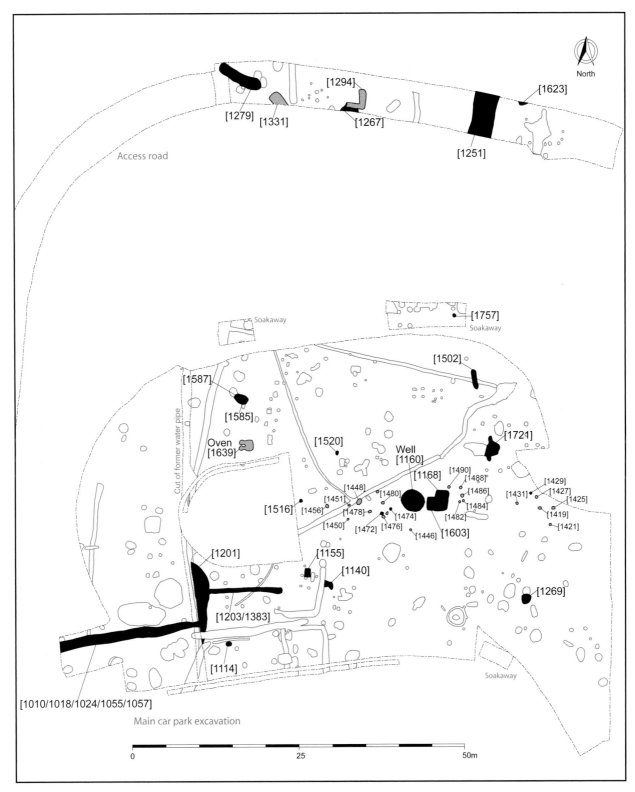

Figure 5. Phase 2 features
(Black = securely dated, grey = poorly dated)

was overlain by a secondary fill containing pottery dating to the second century or later, showing that the shallow upper backfill at the terminus accumulated in a later phase.

Ditch [1010/1018/1024/1055/1057] was up to 1.14 metres wide and 0.5 metres deep. It extended

beyond the edge of the site to the west and joined with [1201]. Although the precise relationship was obscured by a modern water pipe trench, it was almost certainly contemporary as 7 sherds of pottery dated to the late first and early second century were recovered from its fill, as well as 4 undated sherds and a fragment of Roman roof tile.

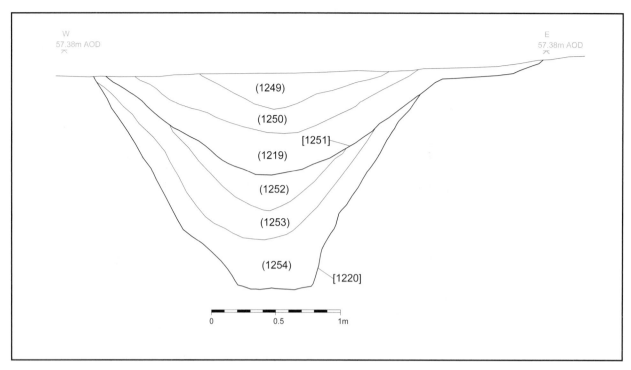

Figure 6. South facing section through ditch [1220] showing re-cut [1251]

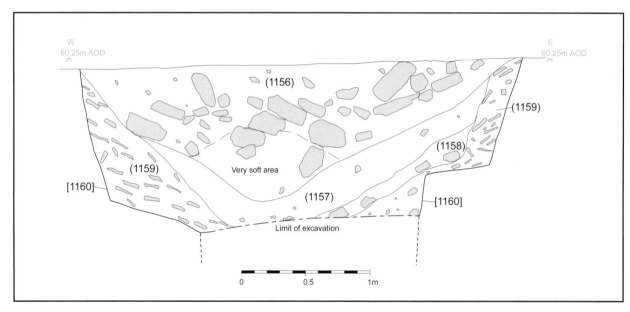

Figure 7. South facing section through well [1160]

Well and clay-lined pits

Three major features investigated within the car park excavation appear to originate in this phase of activity. A large circular vertical-sided cut [1160] was found, with a diameter of 3.6 metres for a depth of approximately 1m. It then stepped in, forming a distinct 'ledge' around 0.6 metres wide. Below this the shaft continued with a diameter of 1.75 metres (Figure 7 and Plate 6). This was only excavated to a maximum depth of 1.30 metres below the surrounding ground level because the shallow depth of foundations needed here would allow the rest of

the feature to be preserved below the car park. As the full depth of the feature was not ascertained a definitive function and date of origin was not determined, but it was almost certain to have been a well.

The upper 'ledge' would have held a masonry lining in exactly the manner of wells 1 and 2 at Dalton Parlours, which although later in date are of almost identical form and dimensions (Wrathmell and Nicholson 1990, Figures 43, 44, 114, 115; Plates XI and XXXV). In this case, as with well 2 at Dalton Parlours, the lining was clearly recovered

Plate 6. Well [1160] showing the upper 'step', looking east

for reuse before backfilling. At greater depth no lining was needed, presumably because the rock-cut sides did not require support and would suffer less wear and tear from drawing water. At Dalton Parlours, the necessity for an upper walled section was explained because, "the more fragmented surface bedrock would otherwise have eroded into the shaft" (Wrathmell and Nicholson 1990, 195).

Although different bedrock, exactly the same observation applies at Nostell.

The dating of this feature is problematic due in part to its unexcavated nature. A single sherd of late first to early second century pottery, abraded and potentially residual in nature, was found in the earliest excavated fill. The later fills contained pottery of a significantly later date indicating that the well

Plate 7. Earlier clay-lined pit [1603] with lining in place, looking south
In this photograph, the later pit has already been excavated above it and the earlier pit is half-sectioned

shaft was filled in the third century or later with the final fill not until the fourth century or later. The actual excavation and use of the well are, naturally, not dated by these deposits, which will have been laid down at the end of the life of the feature. Its attribution to phase 2 is solely based on its proximity to two securely dated clay-lined pits and their obvious water management role.

Less than half a metre to the east of the circular feature were two intercutting shallow, rectangular clay-lined pits [1603] and [1168]. The earlier feature [1603], was orientated east-west, measuring 2.8 metres by 1.85 metres by 0.45 metres deep (Plate 7). It had steep sides and a flat base, lined with a thin layer of soft, pale yellow silty clay. The re-deposited natural backfill of this feature contained 76 sherds of pottery from a single rusticated jar dated between the late first and early or mid second century. This suggests it was deliberately backfilled towards the latter part of phase 2, followed immediately by the construction of the later feature [1168].

The later rectangular clay-lined pit [1168] was orientated north–south, measuring 3.15 metres by 2.3 metres by 0.3 metres deep (Plate 8). It was similar to the earlier feature with steep sides and flat base, and included elements of a clay lining with some flat sandstone slabs apparently set into the clay.

Some of the slabs were slightly reddened, suggesting that they may have been subject to gentle heat although sometimes such discolouration occurs naturally. The surrounding clay into which they were set was soft and did not exhibit any sign of heating, as would probably have occurred during any *in situ* burning. A single sherd of late first to early second century pottery was recovered from this clay. This sherd was abraded, which might suggest that it was residual, but it could still date the feature to this phase. The abrasion might even have derived from the action of whatever water-using activity was being carried out in the pit. The subsequent backfilling of clay (1167), with frequent large slabs and blocks of sandstone and occasional large water-worn cobbles, contained over a hundred sherds of pottery from 23 different vessels, dating the backfilling to the mid to late second century. This suggests that the backfilling of this feature – as distinct, potentially, from its period of use – belongs to phase 3. The backfilling also included an interesting fragment of quern, thought to be the remains of a rare twin-hopper type with military associations typically dating to the second or third century. The sandstone fragments and large cobbles in the backfill may have been the remains of a related superstructure of otherwise unknown form.

Plate 8. Later clay-lined pit [1168], looking north
The backfill of the earlier pit is visible as less rocky ground below and to the left of the photographic scales

Given the presence of the clay lining – well-preserved in the earlier feature, more fragmentary in the later – it seems very likely that both features were designed to hold water (presumably drawn from the adjacent well) and function as broad shallow cisterns. Their shallow nature seems to be deliberate and must relate to the specific activity taking place but beyond this there is little clue to their function. Water-filled pits of this sort may have had industrial uses, or may have been used for the processing of vegetable fibre, or perhaps simply served to water livestock although the design seem over-elaborate and the volume of water too small for the latter.

Posthole group close to the well

Postholes [1474] and [1472] are dated to this period by the pottery in their fills. They lie within 5m to the west of the well and are thus potentially related to the water-holding/using features, as are the surrounding group of otherwise undated postholes [1446], [1448], [1450], [1451], [1456], [1476], [1478], and [1480]. On the other hand, one of this group of otherwise undated postholes, [1458] (Figure 9), contained a counterfeit denarius from the late second to early third century, which dates

its filling to that period or later. This shows that it is necessary to be cautious about assuming all the postholes date to the late first/early second century. As the well itself seems to have continued to be used for many decades, it is also possible that some of the postholes represent later structures associated with it.

Within 2.5 metres of the pits to the east a further group of five small postholes [1482], [1484], [1486], [1488] and [1490] may be related, but only one [1482] contained even a single sherd of pottery, and that broadly dated to the mid second to fourth centuries.

Oven

Excavation in the northwest corner of the main excavation area revealed the sub-structure of an oven or kiln with an unusual double-firebox [1639] (Figure 8 and Plate 9). The main part of this feature comprised an irregular oval cut measuring up to 1.6 metres in diameter and 0.35 metres deep. Two steep sided, flat-based circular cuts were connected to the west side, each measuring 0.6 metres in diameter and 0.35 metres to 0.4 metres deep. The natural sandstone of the western half of the feature, and especially in the two western separate chambers, had been significantly heat affected. The pattern of heat distribution suggested that the larger pit was the stoking area, allowing the oven's operator to tend fires in the two smaller cuts that formed the fireboxes to heat a now absent superstructure. Three small fragments of daub were recovered from the backfills of the feature, but none exhibited signs of direct heat. If they had once been part of this feature's superstructure, this would suggest that parts of it were not subject to intense heat.

The primary fill of both the main cut and the two circular extensions to the feature were rich in charcoal. Examination of a sample taken from this fill revealed the presence of charred cereal grains identified as spelt wheat and barley, together with wood charcoal. A 0.1 metre thick layer

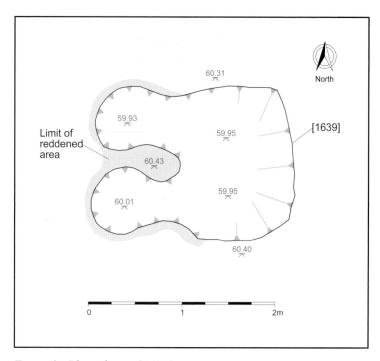

Figure 8. Plan of oven [1639]

of compact brownish-orange silty clay sealed the primary charcoal fill. The colour of this deposit suggested that it might be slightly heat affected, although there is no evidence for high temperature firing resulting in a recognisable structure or hardening in the clay. This clay might represent a col-

lapsed superstructure of the feature, or alternatively a deliberately dumped backfill, slightly heated by underlying, still warm, charcoal. If this interpretation is correct then the feature was backfilled immediately after the oven's final use. The majority of the feature had been backfilled with clayey sand

Plate 9. Oven [1639], looking west

containing frequent sandstone fragments derived from the local bedrock. Radiocarbon dating of the charred material recovered from the primary fill of the main part of this feature provided a date range of 70 – 230 Cal.AD with a 95% probability (Beta Analytic 2012). However, there was a 68% probability that the date lay between 80 and 140 Cal. AD suggesting it may date to this phase of the site although there is no artefactual evidence to support this.

Interpretation of this feature is made difficult by the absence of the superstructure that would have covered the two fire-boxes. The cereal grains present in the charcoal rich fill might indicate the kind of activity that was taking place here suggesting that this was an oven associated with either food preparation or agricultural activity. Although this is far from the typical form of a corn-drier (see discussion section), the assemblage of charred grain could be consistent with that usage. Nothing was found to indicate that a higher-temperature industrial process was taking place here.

Postholes and pits in the southern part of the main car park

Posthole [1429], about 15 metres east of the well, was dated to the late first to early second century. It was part of a roughly rectangular cluster of six postholes with [1419], [1421], [1425], [1427] and [1431], which averaged only 0.1m in depth. The layout is not quite regular enough to represent a building but they may be part of a larger structure lying beyond the edge of excavation to the northeast.

To the south of that posthole group, pit [1269] also contained pottery from this period and lay equidistant to the southeast of the well.

Two isolated postholes [1520] and [1516] contained late first to early second century pottery in their single fills. They were respectively 10m northwest and 15m west of the well, and a little way beyond the associated group of postholes.

A single isolated posthole in the southwest part of the main car park [1114] and two small pits [1155] and [1140] were also dated to this phase of activity on the basis of their pottery content.

Features to the north of the main car park and in the access road

Excavation within the northern area of the main car park revealed several pits [1585], [1587], [1721] that dated to this phase although no definitive function could be assigned to any of these features. In the case of pit [1721] this dating is on the basis of a single abraded sherd that may be residual, while the pit was so irregular that it may also have been heavily disturbed by tree roots. Pits [1587] and [1585] were intercutting, though it was impossible to tell which cut which. The pits contained in their single fill 78 sherds from a near complete honey pot of Flavian-Trajanic (69-117) date. Pit [1587] cut a circular posthole [1677], which contained no dating evidence but must date to this phase or to the pre-Roman Iron Age phase (not labelled on Figure 4 or 5).

The soakaway trench just to the north of this area, also contained a number of postholes and pits but no obvious pattern in the layout of these features was evident within soakaway trench or in the main excavation area immediately to the south. Interpretation was also hindered by the paucity of dating evidence, which was limited to a single small sherd of pottery probably dated to the first century, recovered from posthole [1757].

Additional features, which appear to originate in this phase, were identified in the access road. Postholes [1205] and [1240] each contained a single sherd of abraded early Roman pottery, but the features appeared to be more closely related to a corn-drier of a later date, suggesting the postholes may also be later in date and the pottery they contained residual (see Figures 9 and 10). An irregular pit or disturbed posthole [1267] contained a body sherd from a probable glazed beaker of late first or early second century date as well as other pottery of similar date. This irregular pit or posthole was cut by the southern edge of an L-shaped cut [1294]. This comprised two lengths of ditch, V-shaped in profile, 0.8 metres wide and up to 0.36 metres deep, aligned east-west and north-south, meeting at the southeast corner. Each of the two components was 2.85 metres in length. A single fill was excavated, which contained occasional sherds of very abraded undiagnostic Romano-British pottery. This feature could date from the early Roman phase or later ones.

Phase 3: Mid to late second century AD

Pottery dating predominantly from the mid to late second century defined this phase of activity. Evidence of a change in the sources of pottery supply from those of the earlier phases may indicate a discontinuity in either pottery supply or the nature of occupation during the first half of the second century. The pottery types found in this and later phases lack the specifically military aspect of the

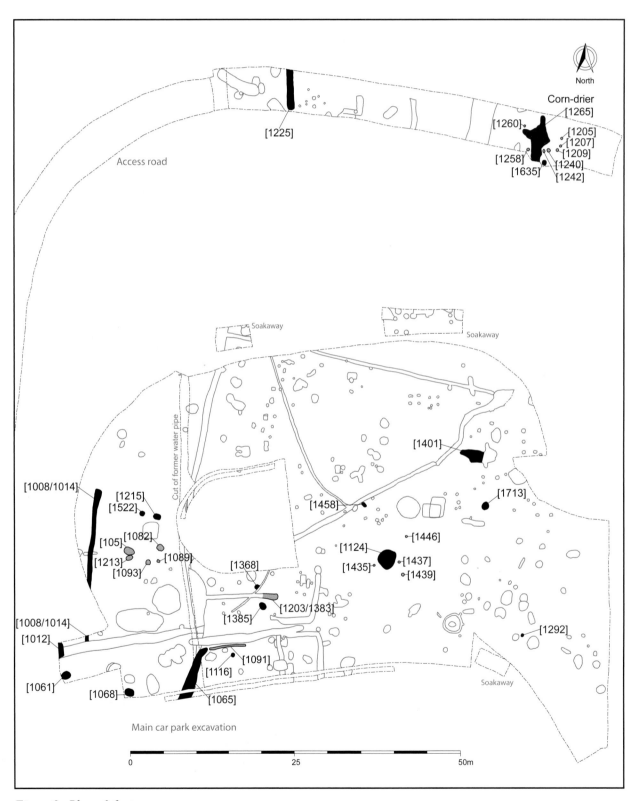

Figure 9. Phase 3 features
(Black = securely dated, grey = poorly dated)

early Roman phase, suggesting a 'clean break' from the previous phase. Further land divisions in the form of ditches were formed in the southwest part of the car park area, sometimes using or respecting the earlier landscape. New activity in this phase is represented by the excavation of several pits in the southwest quadrant of the site (setting a pattern that would continue in phase 4 as well), and also by the presence of a corn-drier in the access road (Figure 9).

Land divisions

Further ditches [1008/1014] and [1065], dating to this phase of occupation of the site, were found in the western part in the main car park area. The north-south aligned ditch [1008/1014] contained a small amount of pottery in its fill dated (at the latest) to the mid second century, and the southern end of it terminated just short of, thus appearing to respect, the east-west aligned ditch [1010/1018/1024/1055/1057] that dated to phase 2. This indicated that the earlier ditch was still recognisable – and was perhaps still in use - as a boundary despite being substantially backfilled. As there was no stratigraphic relationship between the two, it is also possible that [1008/1014] was open at a much earlier date and formed part of a boundary with [1010/1018/1024/1055/1057], but was backfilled at a later date.

The north-northeast to south-southwest aligned ditch terminus [1065], located at the southern edge of the excavation and extending beyond its limits, contained a small quantity of second century pottery and cut through the backfilled earlier ditch [1201]. A very slight, narrow east-west aligned gully [1091] only measuring 5.5 metres in length, to the east of this ditch, may represent a shallower continuation of this feature, although it lacked any precise dating evidence other than mid second to fourth century pottery.

Pottery dating from the second century or later was also recovered from the upper fill of the early Roman ditch [1203/1383] to the north, running parallel to the narrow gully, demonstrating that the upper part of this ditch terminus was open, although only to a relatively shallow depth, until backfilled in this phase.

In the access road a narrow, north-south aligned ditch [1225], which terminated close to the southern limits of this excavated area, was dated to this period by pottery recovered from its primary and upper fills. Close by, a heavily truncated, irregular north-south aligned plough furrow [1222] is of much later date (not shown on Figure 9), despite a small number of abraded Romano-British pottery sherds being recovered from it, and is further evidence of medieval ploughing that has been found elsewhere in the vicinity.

Pits in the southwest quadrant of the main car park and other nearby activity

This phase also appears to represent a change in the focus of activity encountered on the site. Three pits [1012], [1061] and [1068] with pottery dated to this period in their backfills were found in the southwest corner of the site, an area that had not contained features of this type in earlier phases. The pits were typically oval, measuring approximately 1.5 metres across at most and appear to contain deliberate single backfills. The pits may have served as rubbish pits or had an unknown function before being backfilled. Pit [1061] contained occasional fragments of burnt sandstone, but this offered little clue to its function. However, many of the other pits within this area contained pottery of third century date and have been therefore ascribed to the next phase. It is possible that the relatively small quantity of second century pottery recovered from these pits is residual and that these pits therefore also belong to the later phase. This was the case with pit [1034]. Despite containing phase 3 pottery it was stratigraphically later than a phase 4 pit (Figure 11). On the other hand, it is certainly possible that these three pits are second century in date and that the pattern of site use in this area established in this phase continued into the next.

To the north of these pits two large postholes, [1215] and [1522], containing pottery dated to the mid to late second century appeared to form the northern side of a rectangular structure measuring roughly 6.4 metres by 2.9 metres. Otherwise undated postholes [1093] and [1213], of a similar size and shape, formed the southern end of the rectangular structure, while the very shallow postholes to the east, [1082] and [1089], may also be related. (A further pit to the west, excavated during the trial trenching as [105], may also have been part of this structure, although it was notably larger and might not be contemporary.) Although spatially pit [1218] appeared to lie within the structure the infilling of the pit was dated later, to the third and fourth century (Figure 12). This shows that this apparent relationship was coincidental as it is unlikely that the otherwise unremarkable pit would have been in use until backfilled up to two hundred years later.

Excavation towards the southern area of the main car park uncovered a number of postholes and small pits. Six sherds of an early to mid second century rusticated jar were in the single fill of posthole [1116]. Posthole [1385] and a pit [1368] contained undiagnostic Romano-British pottery but these features did not form a coherent group or purpose and were within an area of numerous undated features of a similar sort.

Pit in east part of the car park area and nearby posthole group

A large oval pit [1124] measuring approximately 2.5 metres in diameter and 0.23 metres deep, located to the southeast of the centre of the main excavated area, also appears to represent activity dating from this phase. The pit had no clearly defined function but the single backfill deposit contained 30 sherds of pottery, the latest of which was dated to the mid to late second century and included the remains of a lattice decorated black-burnished ware jar. Four small truncated postholes ([1435], [1437], [1439] and [1446]) in the vicinity appear to be associated with the pit – perhaps supporting a light roof or windbreak - but the only dating evidence was from the single fill of [1446] in the form of 5 sherds of undiagnostic shell tempered ware of either Iron Age or Romano-British date.

A single large isolated posthole [1713], incorporating a sandstone pad stone, sandstone packing and a recognisable post-pipe, was also found. A small assemblage of pottery dated to this period was recovered from the fill around the pad stone.

An oval pit [1401], measuring up to 2.1 metres in length and 0.55 metres deep was located to the north of the above features. The steep sided, flat-based pit cut through the fill of the earlier, phase 2, irregular pit [1721] and contained three fills. The primary fill contained frequent charcoal and ash.

Examination of a sample taken from this primary fill indicated the presence of large fragments of softwood charcoal together with weed seeds but little evidence for crop grains. There was no evidence that the natural sandstone into which the pit had been dug was heat affected; therefore the charcoal rich initial fill must have been deposited from elsewhere and not burnt *in situ*. Several sherds of pottery dating to the second century were also recovered from this primary fill and the backfill deposits contained pottery sherds, including samian ware, dated to the mid to late second century.

An isolated posthole [1292] in the far eastern part of the main car park contained two sherds of pottery possibly dated to the mid second to mid third century.

Corn-drier and associated postholes

Situated in the access road area was a corn-drier [1265] (Figure 10 and Plate 10). The feature comprised of an irregular polygonal cut measuring up to 6.2 metres by 4.2 metres and 0.36 metres deep. The main part of the cut was broadly rectangular, measuring 2.8 metres from northwest to southeast, and 2.6 metres from northeast to southwest. An irregular western offshoot extended approximately 1 metre from the main body of the feature.

The north and south parts of the cut were better defined and included possible structural remains, as described below, forming the two lined flues. The northern section extended approximately 1.4 metres from the main part of the feature, with an average width of 0.65 metres. The bedrock was overlain along the base of this section by a thin layer of firm pinkish-orange, heat-affected, sandy clay (1263), which included, along its edges, several fragments of burnt sandstone that appeared to have originally formed a lining. A dish sherd dated to the mid second to third century was recovered from this clay deposit as well as a very corroded Roman copper brooch. In the space between the eastern edge of the stones in this deposit and the outside edge of the cut a backfill deposit of orange grey clay sand (1305), containing frequent fragments of naturally derived sandstone had been placed and was likely to be part of the original construction of this feature. It contained 11 fragments of second century pottery. The southern section extended

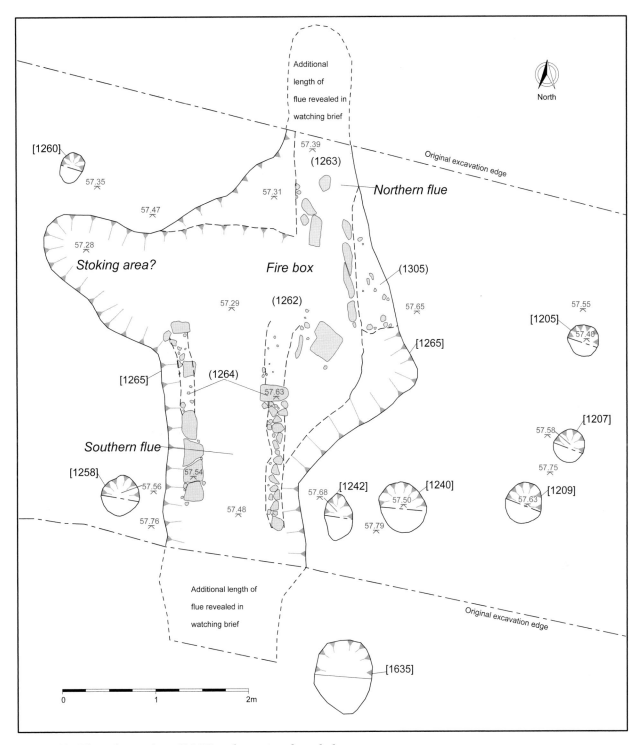

Figure 10. Plan of corn-drier [1265] and associated postholes

beyond the edge of excavation, a distance of over 2 metres, and was wider, at almost 1.5 metres. A better preserved stone lining (1264) was recorded in the southern section. This comprised small sub-angular sandstone blocks, a maximum of 250 mm across, bonded with firm yellow clay, forming two parallel lines with an internal gap of 0.7 metres.

Close to the junction of the two lined flues, an ash-rich deposit of dark grey brown clay silt (1262), containing frequent small fragments of burnt stone

and charcoal flecks, was excavated. This deposit contained pottery dated to the mid to late second century and two very small fragments of glass. A sample of this deposit was processed and examined and was shown to contain substantial quantities of well preserved cereal grains, identified as spelt wheat, free threshing wheat and hulled barley and well preserved spelt wheat chaff. Several types of wild plants, which are commonly classed as crop weeds, were also present. The environmental evi-

Plate 10. Recording corn-drier [1265], looking northwest

dence supported the interpretation that this feature was a form of corn-drier although – as is sometimes the case with these features – the precise method of operation was opaque. It is probable that the area containing the ash rich deposit was the fire-box, serving raised floors above both the northern and southern stone-lined flues. The irregular western offshoot of the main cut may have been the stoking area for the fire allowing the flames to be tended and the ash to be raked out.

The majority of the feature was backfilled with mid grey brown sandy silt (1261), which contained occasional fragments of sandstone and flecks of charcoal, together with a mixed assemblage of pottery, ranging in date from late first /early second century to as late as the third. The pottery assemblage from the corn-drier as a whole suggests that, "this feature was being used during the second half of the second

century and fell out of use by the third century" (Leary, this volume). The backfill also contained a small copper fitting with glass inlay in heavily decayed condition.

A number of postholes [1205], [1207], [1209], [1240], [1242], [1258], [1260] and [1635] were present close to the structure forming a line enclosing its southern part and extending north on both sides. While the bulk of the postholes were undated or contained undiagnostic Romano-British pottery, [1635] contained pottery from this phase, and two, [1205] and [1240], contained single sherds from the early Roman phase. However the close physical association of the posthole group to the corn-drier makes it most likely that the early pottery was residual, especially as it was either abraded or very abraded, and that all the postholes are part of a structure covering or sheltering – in the form of a wind break - the corn-drier. It may be that the postholes related to further undiscovered examples beyond the southern trench edge to make a more coherent structure.

Phase 4: Third century AD

This phase is defined by the presence of pottery fabrics common in the third century. This period saw a continuation of pit digging in the southwest quadrant of site and a hiatus in land division although some of the small-scale boundaries back-

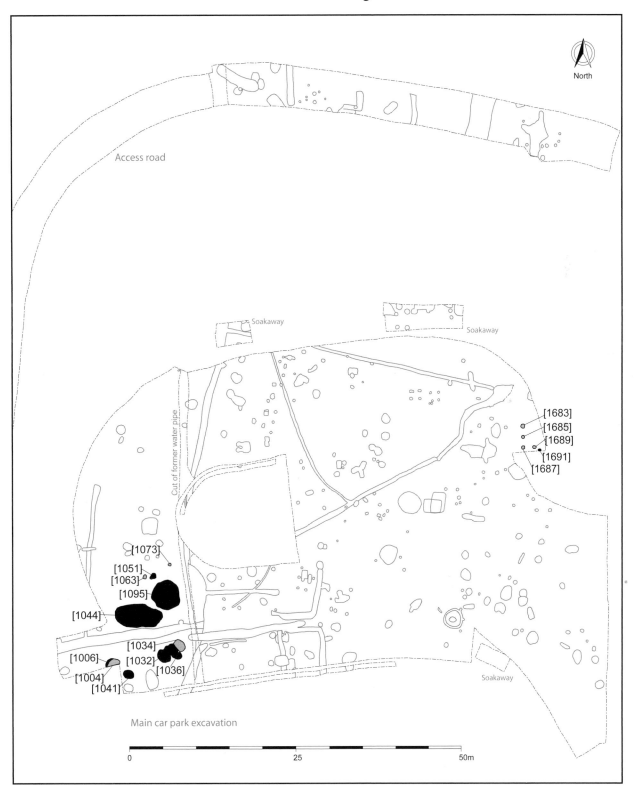

Figure 11. Phase 4 features
(Black = securely dated, grey = poorly dated)

filled in phase 5 may have been open and in use in the third century (Figure 11).

Pits in the southwest quadrant of the main car park

As with the previous phase there is a distinct focus of activity in the southwest corner of the site, represented by a cluster of pits [1006], [1032], [1036], and [1041] dated by third to fourth century pottery. They all also contained rare to occasional burnt sandstone and cobbles. A further pit, [1004], contained occasional burnt stones but no datable artefacts; it did, though, cut through phase 4 pit [1006] and must therefore date to either this phase or phase 5. Pit [1034] cut the fill of pit [1036], which means that despite containing residual pottery of phase 3 date it must belong to this phase or later. These pits appear to have been deliberately backfilled, possibly with domestic refuse, therefore suggesting an element of continuity with the pits in the same area dating from the mid to late second century (if these have been correctly dated).

Also located in this southwest corner and dating to this phase were two very large shallow oval pits [1095] and [1044], both with irregular gently sloping sides and flat or slightly uneven bases. The easterly of these pits [1095] had a maximum diameter of 4.35 metres and a maximum depth of 0.35 metres. The primary fill comprised of sand and frequent fragments of locally derived sandstone but no artefacts. The feature had subsequently been backfilled with sand and silt containing a large number of burnt cobbles and fragments of sandstone (some of which had been burnt) together with nine fragments of pottery, the latest of which were dated to the third century.

The kind of burnt cobbles found in this pit and others from this area in both phase 3 and this phase are sometimes described as 'pot boilers'. While such stones are effective at heating water or liquid food by being placed into a cooking vessel, in reality they could have had a number of purposes, and it is impossible to be certain of their function.

The second shallow oval pit [1044] lay immediately to the southwest. It measured 7.1 metres by 3.3 metres with a maximum depth of 0.5 metres. A single sherd of South Yorkshire Grey Ware pottery, dating from the second to fourth century, was recov-

ered from its sandy primary fill (1047). Fifty-seven sherds of pottery ranging in date from the late first, second and third centuries were recovered from the upper fill (1027) of silty sand as well as occasional pieces of burnt stone. No definitive function could be assigned to these irregular features, but the relatively large amount of broken pottery and the heated stone 'potboilers' may be indicative of their end use for rubbish disposal. To the north of the large pits a single posthole [1051], containing a single sherd of pottery dated to the third century, lay with two further undated postholes [1063] and [1073] that may have been contemporary with it.

Structure in the east of main car park area

On the extreme eastern edge of the main excavation were five substantial postholes [1683], [1685], [1687], [1689] and [1691], each between 0.4m and 0.55m across, which were thought likely to be contemporary due to the similarity of their shapes. Three of these formed a north south line, with the other two to the east of its south end, suggesting an L-shaped structure, or the southwest corner of a rectangle that continued beyond the edge of excavation to the east. One of these [1691] contained a single sherd of pottery dated to the 3rd century.

Phase 5: Late third – fourth century AD

Pottery dating from the late third century to the early/mid fourth century defined the last Romano-British phase of the site (Figure 12). Imprecision in known dates of pottery of the type in the assemblage means that there is the possibility that elements of this phase actually overlap with the later part of the earlier phase, as will be noted below.

Pits in the southwest quadrant of the main car park

Continuing in the pattern of the previous two phases, three pits were located in the southwest corner of the main car park. Pit [1030] contained pottery in its upper fill that dated to the late third to mid fourth century, and cut through two of the pits from phase 4. Like the pits assigned to the earlier phases, it appears to have been deliberately backfilled possibly with domestic refuse.

Pit [1218] was dated by pottery to this phase of activity. The sub-square pit measured approximately 2.5 metres in width and 0.9 metres in depth with

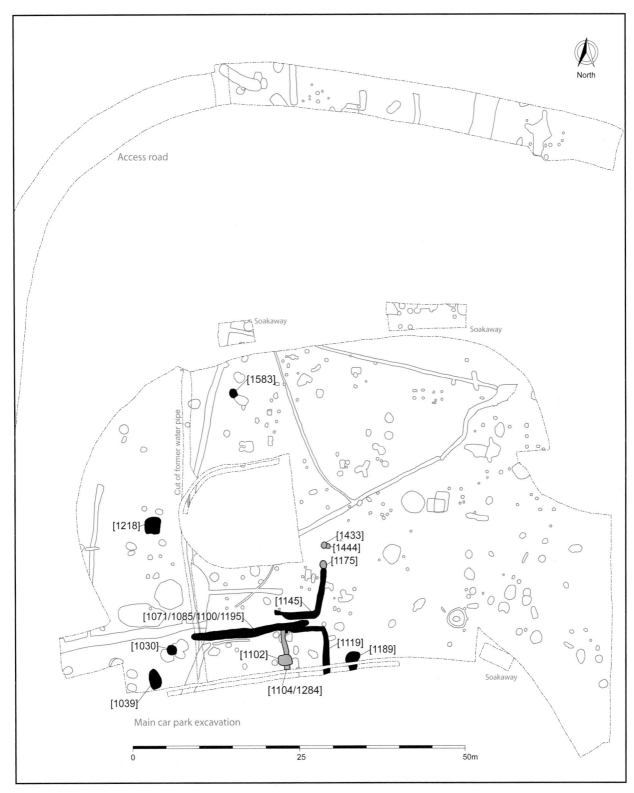

Figure 12. Phase 5 features
(Black = securely dated, grey = poorly dated)

steep sides and a flat base. The primary shallow fills, which appeared to be a result of the erosion of the pit sides, were sealed by probably deliberate backfill deposits of sand and sandstone containing metal working waste. This included three lumps of slag of the type which would have collected in the smith's hearth, known as 'smithing hearth bottoms' and a small quantity of flake hammer scale - small flakes of scale dislodged from the metal surface during smithing (Mortimer 2011). There was no evidence to suggest the pit itself was directly related to metalworking although it is likely that smithing had been undertaken in the immediate vicinity. A further backfill deposit of sand and sandstone contained six fragments of a flanged bowl from the mid third century or later. At the top of the backfill was a distinctive lens of dark bluish black silty sand containing fifteen fragments of pottery, the most recent of which dated to the late third or fourth century.

A further pit, also containing metal working debris, was found to the south. This large pit [1039] was also dated by pottery to the late third or fourth century. It measured 3 metres in diameter and contained a single deposit, which appeared to represent deliberate backfill. The single fill of this probable rubbish pit contained a collection of fuel ash slag indicative of plant ash reacting with a furnace lining during a high temperature process (Mortimer 2011).

Four of five known smithing hearth bottoms were found in features dated to this phase, three from pit [1218] and one from the upper fill of ditch [1071/1085/1100/1195] (the final example was in an undated posthole). Although this would seem to suggest that small-scale ironworking was taking place for the first time in this phase the quantities are not substantial and it may reflect the clearance of earlier metalworking debris from an earlier phase. No features directly relating to smithing were found.

Land divisions

Several additional ditches are also thought to date to this phase of activity, including two L-shaped ditches [1119] and [1145]. Ditch [1119], measuring 0.7 metres to 1 metre wide and 0.20 metres deep (Plate 11), extended northwards from the

Plate 11. Ditch [1119], looking south

southern limit of excavation before turning to the west and continuing for a further 4.5 metres. The ditch generally contained sandy silt and sandstone backfill deposits with a variety of pottery sherds, the latest of which was dated to the mid third to fourth century. Unavoidable imprecision in the pottery dating means that this ditch could in fact have been filled in the later part of phase 4. Immediately to the north of [1119] was a second L-shaped ditch [1145] of similar dimensions and appearing to mirror [1119] suggesting the two are likely to be contemporary although there were no datable artefacts from ditch [1145] apart from a scrap of Romano-British pottery.

At the northern end of ditch [1145] there was a substantial posthole [1175] measuring 1 metre in diameter and 0.7 metres deep. So close is the physical association between the two features that they are likely to have been contemporary (Plate 12). The posthole contained occasional very large sandstone blocks (up to 500mm in length) that had been set in an upright position to form packing, although no finds were recovered from the fill. To the north was a posthole of similar size and also packed with sandstone blocks [1433], which may be contemporary and related to the other posthole and L-shaped ditch. The fills of this posthole included a large recognisable post-pipe deposit, which contained sherds of pottery, probable calcite gritted ware dating to the late third to early fifth century. Posthole [1433] had cut through another large posthole

Plate 13. Ditch [1071/1085/1100/1195], looking east

[1444], which was at least 0.85 across and 0.4m deep, but did not include any obvious post pipe or finds in its fill. This may represent the replacement of the earlier post.

The L-shaped ditches are suggestive of a corral entrance, funnelling animals from the east towards the west, with the large postholes to the north marking the start of a fence perhaps continued with more ephemeral posts that have not survived. However a further east-west aligned ditch [1071/1085/1100/1195] recorded for a total length of 17.5 metres and measuring up to 1.2 metres wide and 0.45 metres deep was later located within – and effectively closed off - the postulated entrance formed by the two L-shaped ditches (Plate 13). In its upper fill were found 190 pieces of pottery (the latest dating to the late third to early fourth century date), a fragment of glass waste, a couple of brick or tile fragments and 17 pieces of daub. A single smithing hearth bottom was also recovered from the upper fill of this ditch, as was a fragment of rotary quern. The ditch's presence shows that the spatial organisation of the site was still being adapted in this final phase of Romano-British occupation.

Ditch [1071/1085/1100/1195] also cut a nearby ditch [1104/1284], which was aligned north-south and continued beyond the southern limit of excavation, a total length of 5m lying within the excavated area. It was 0.6m wide and a maximum of 0.19m deep. The single fill (1103/1283) of reddish brown sandy-clay-silt contained a sherd of third century or later black-burnished ware with lattice decoration

Plate 12. Posthole [1175] and terminus of ditch [1145], looking south

and four fragments of Roman brick or tile. Its position is suggestive of association with the L-shaped ditch [1119], perhaps forming a small enclosure but this is speculative and it might equally be an unrelated boundary from the earlier phase. It was cut by a large pit [1102], which contained pottery of the third century or later and which, if the dating of ditch [1104/1284] is correct, must date to this phase.

A further feature, [1189], located at the southern limit of excavation and also recorded within a soakaway trench to the south, contained pottery of this phase. The extension of the feature to the south, within the soakaway trench, suggests that it may be the terminus of a ditch possibly related to ditch [1071/1085/1100/1195] 'blocking' the earlier entrance. Its fill (1188) contained several sherds of pottery, ranging in date from the late first/second century, to the late third/fourth century.

Well

The only other feature excavated that contained pottery of this date was the previously discussed well [1160]. The earliest excavated fill of this feature included a single scrap of, probably residual, pottery dating to the earliest phase of Romano-British activity but subsequent fills contain much later pottery and the final upper fill is firmly dated by pottery to the early to mid fourth century. The presence in the upper fill of pottery dating to three centuries later, together with the absence of intersection of other features during intervening phases, suggests that the well was still open, and presumably in use to some extent, throughout the entire period covered by the Romano-British occupation of the site, and may not have been backfilled until the fourth century.

Other features

A single large isolated posthole [1583] in the north part of the main excavation dated to this phase.

Undated or unphased features (Iron-Age or Romano-British)

A number of features lacked either datable finds or stratigraphic relationships to enable them to be placed securely within any specific phase of activity (Figure 13). These included possible burials, four-post grain stores and further land divisions. Numerous postholes and pits were also not dated. Those that formed clear, regular, groups are discussed either here (if undated) or in the phased sections above (when one or more of a group are dated, or an obvious association with a dated feature occurs).

Unphased Romano-British boundaries, posthole alignments and pits

In the northern part of the car park two alignments of postholes originally formed fences orientated roughly north-northeast to south-southwest, which are probably Romano-British in date but not attributable to a specific phase. The southern end of the eastern alignment begins with two large rectangular intercutting postholes [1669] and [1671]. These were 0.7-0.75 metres across and 0.3-0.35 metres deep, with steep sides and flat bases. The eastern alignment continued with three square or rectangular postholes [1661], [1659] and [1596] each a maximum of 0.35 metres across and 0.1-0.2 metres deep, set at regular intervals of approximately 1.4 metres. After a gap of 3.7 metres the alignment continued, with a further five postholes [1621], [1607], [1611], [1613] and [1627], which were rectangular and oval, between 0.25 and 0.4 metres across, and 0.12-0.24 metres deep and spaced at approximately 1.4 metre intervals. Two of the postholes [1611] and [1613] were intercutting indicating that an earlier post had been replaced.

The second posthole alignment lay just over 1 metre to the west of the first. It comprised a total of eight rectangular, square and oval postholes [1663], [1665], [1667], [1641], [1637], [1581], [1631] and [1633], each between 0.35 and 0.9 metres across and 0.15-0.5 metres deep. The spacing along this alignment was slightly less regular than in that to the east, and in one instance a posthole had been replaced (posthole [1665] cut [1667]).

The posthole alignments contained no precisely datable pottery, just single indeterminate scraps of

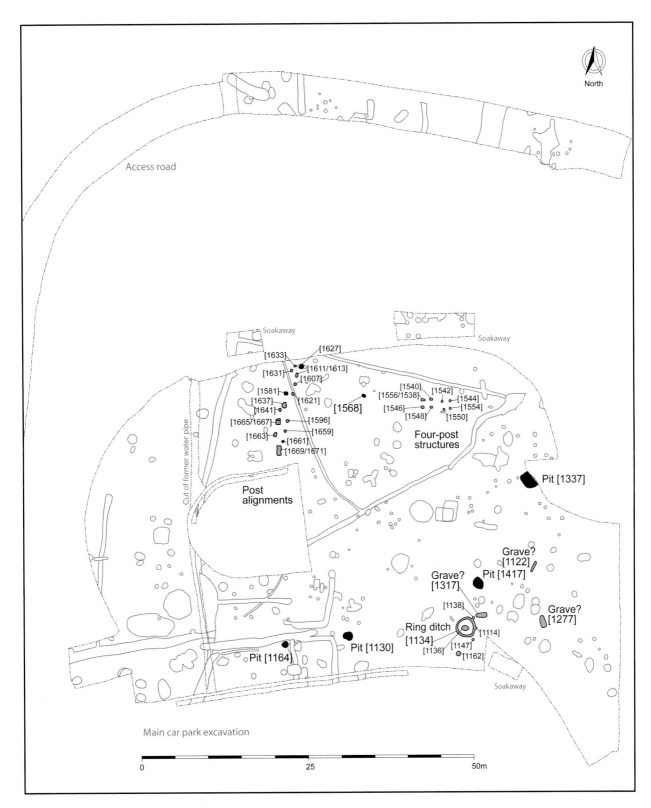

Figure 13. Undated or unphased features
(Black = containing Romano-British pottery, grey = no dating evidence)

Roman pottery from the fills of [1627] and [1661] and a fragment of pottery dating from 120 AD or later in the single fill of [1581]. The rows of postholes appear to roughly continue the line of a boundary represented by phase 3 ditch [1065] to the south, although the two features were separated by some distance. The lines are also parallel to the

course of the earlier ditch [1496] thought to be pre-Roman in date, which does not necessarily mean the postholes are contemporary with it but that this ditch (or an associated bank) was still sufficiently visible in the landscape to influence the organisation of the later boundary.

Other features that contained Romano-British pottery of non-specific date included a posthole [1568] in the north part of the main car park and a pit [1130] in the southern part, which again contained single scraps of undiagnostic pottery. One fragment of box-flue tile was identified from the fill of an oval pit [1164], probably dating the feature to the Romano-British period although the box flue is impossible to attribute to a particular phase. Towards the east area of the main car park excavation, a pit [1417], within an area of largely undated similar features, contained a fragment of Romano-British pottery and further to the north pottery in a single large pit [1337] was dated from the mid second century or later.

Possible burials and funerary monuments

Perhaps the most significant group of undated features comprised possible funerary activity located towards the eastern limits of the main excavated area. The difficulty in confirming this interpretation is due to the complete absence of bone (animal or human) surviving in any of these features (and, indeed, across the vast majority of the site). The reason for this is not well understood. Normally bone is eroded in acid conditions, but at Nostell the soils are alkaline enough to support a healthy earthworm population. The phenomenon is known from other sites on coal measures-type sandstone bedrock and may be the result of some other element of geological chemistry.

Two shallow features [1277] and [1317], measuring 0.3 metres deep were considered to be possible graves due to their sub-rectangular shape and dimensions of 1.85 and 1.7 metres in length and 0.7 and 0.8 metres in width. The fills of these features contained no traces of bone or artefact material. Similarly sized features were found at the Romano-British rural settlement of Thurnscoe in South Yorkshire, where they were interpreted as 'empty' Romano-British graves (Neal and Fraser 2004).

A possible small stone-lined grave [1122] was also found nearby (Figure 14 and Plate 14). The cut of this grave [1122] was sub-rectangular, orientated south-southwest to north-northeast measuring a maximum of 1.4 metres long, 0.5 metres wide and had a maximum depth of 0.2 metres. The feature had a flat base and the sides of the cut were very

steep or vertical, lined with edge-lain sandstone slabs up to 400mm in width. A spread of sandstone rubble on the west side of the cut may have been collapsed or plough-damaged lining, or possibly a substantially ploughed-out cairn. The fill within the lining consisted of clayey sandy silt containing oc-

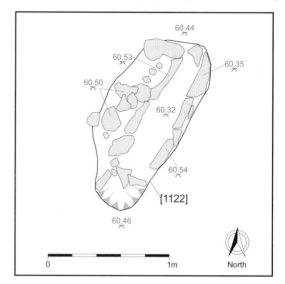

Figure 14. Plan of stone-lined 'grave' [1122]

casional pebbles and small fragments of sandstone, but no artefacts or bone. Given the dimensions of this feature, the presence of the lining and possible ploughed out cairn, a tentative interpretation as the grave of a child seems plausible although proof is denied by the lack of bone. Similar partially stone-lined graves are known from Parlington Hollins near Aberford (Roberts, Burgess & Berg 2001), where they were dated to the late Roman, or possibly even the sub-Roman, period.

In the course of the evaluation phase of the investigation, a near-complete Roman handled jar of South Yorkshire type was found upright in a scoop in the natural ground surface approximately 10m north east of stone-lined grave [1122] (see Plate 16). The vessel was in approximately 40 fragments and was impossible to date closely; it may have been late second to third century, but potentially was of as wide a range as mid-second century to mid fourth century. Although there was no direct evidence that the pot was related to the 'burials', it is unusual to find complete vessels, let alone one set upright in place. One possible scenario is that the pot held mortuary-related offerings or votive deposits, but this is purely speculative, based on the vessel's approximate proximity to the 'burial' features. The vessel contained no physical trace of an offering

Plate 14. Stone-lined 'child's grave' [1122], looking north

or of bone, cremated or otherwise. The former, especially in the protected environment of the vessel would almost certainly have survived had it ever been present.

The final possible funerary monument, located just to the southwest of the possible graves described above, consisted of a small, narrow, circular ring ditch [1134] (Figure 15). This had a maximum external diameter of 3 metres with the ditch measuring up to 0.35 metres wide and 0.14 metres deep. The ditch contained a single sandy clay and sandstone deposit, with frequent small fragments of natural sandstone, but no artefacts. Towards the centre of the ring ditch was an oval pit [1136], measuring 1.1 metres by 0.7 metres wide by 0.12 metres deep. Its sandy clay fill did not contain any traces of bone or artefacts. The outside of the eastern edge of the ring ditch was cut by two circular postholes [1138] and [1149], which together with a similar posthole

[1147] located to the south, appeared to form an arc around the ring ditch. This was possibly continued to the south by posthole [1162] although this was considerably larger. (See the Discussion section possible interpretations of this ring ditch.)

Four-post structures and other features

Two other undated structures excavated to the north of the main car park are also likely to relate to the Iron Age or Romano-British phases of activity. These comprised two small square "four-post structures" both approximately 1.2 metres square, formed by two groups of shallow postholes [1538/1540/1546/1548] (Plate 15) and [1542/1544/1550/1554]. In the first example [1538] replaced an earlier posthole [1556] through which it cut. None of the postholes contained any finds but "four-post structures" of this kind are frequently present on rural sites of Iron-Age and

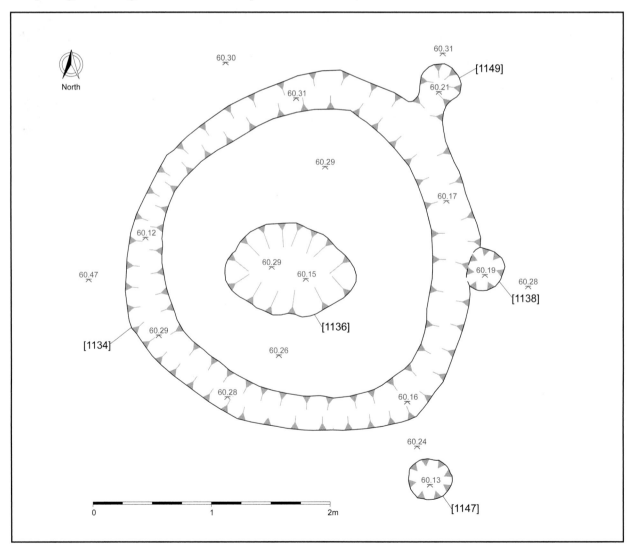

Figure 15. Plan of ring ditch [1134] and associated postholes

Romano-British date and are usually interpreted as granaries with a suspended storage floor raised on posts allowing air circulation while keeping the grain safe from animal pests or damp. Two similar postholes [1552] and [1558] (shown but not labelled on Figure 13) were located immediately adjacent to the southwest corner of the second structure. Adjacent postholes of this sort have been interpreted as the base of ladders (e.g. Van de Noort 2007).

Plate 15. Four-post structure [1538/1540/1546/1548] looking west

Part 3

The Artefacts and Environmental Evidence

3.1 The Romano-British pottery

Ruth Leary

Introduction

The pottery was examined in context groups and catalogued according to the Guidelines of the Study Group for Romano-British Pottery for basic archiving (Darling 2004). The fabrics were recorded in broad groups and source suggested where appropriate. Reference was made to the National Fabric Collection where appropriate (Tomber and Dore 1998). Details of fabric variations were recorded where appropriate. Vessel forms were described.

There were 2019 sherds of Romano-British pottery (c29kg.) and 23 sherds of handmade pottery (228g) dating to the pre-Roman Iron Age (PRIA) or early Roman period.

Wares

The fabric of the pottery was first examined by eye and sorted into ware groups on the basis of colour, hardness, feel, fracture, inclusions and manufacturing technique. If the sherds could not be adequately grouped by eye then they were examined under an x30 binocular microscope and compared with sherds from known sources. National fabric collection codes are given wherever possible (Tomber and Dore 1998). Table 2 shows the pottery fabric codes used in this report along with a brief description of the fabric and a note on its source. Table 3 tabulates the contents of the pottery assemblage, including the samian pottery and the mortaria, which are reported on separately (Monteil and Hartley, this volume). Note that the early grey, white and oxidised wares included sherds that had been fired to the "wrong" colour or to several colours and this demonstrated that the fabrics were the same basic clay.

The Romano-British types of fabrics and forms identified in the assemblage date from the Flavian period to the early fourth century. Two major periods of activity - phases 2 and 3 - can be identified, one in the Flavian or Flavian-Trajanic period (69-96AD or 69-117AD) and one in the mid to late second century. Continuation into the third and fourth centuries (phases 4 and 5) is indicated by later types, such as the small numbers of Dales ware sherds, BB1 splayed-rim jars, hammerhead and multi-reeded rim mortaria, a late Nene Valley colour-coated vessel and one pre-Huntcliff jar rim.

Phase 1: Pre-Roman Iron Age (PRIA)

Two near complete PRIA vessels were identified. These may date to the late Iron Age or early Roman period since, in this region, handmade vessels of PRIA type continued to be used on rural sites as late as the early second century. One small jar in a coarse quartz tempered ware had a small rounded, slightly turned out rim while another was necked with a finely made everted rim tip and scoring on the shoulder and surviving upper body. The former vessel is a common form through the Iron Age and early Roman period while scoring on the latter suggests a link with the later Iron Age scored ware of the East Midlands. The finely made neck and rim also point towards a late date, in the late PRIA or early Roman period. It is very unlikely that these two pots were used by the same people who used the fully Romanised vessels of Flavian-Trajanic type and these are more likely to represent pre-Flavian activity on the site. On the other hand it is possible that a fully Roman settlement might acquire such vessels because of their contents.

Phase 2: Flavian-Trajanic period (69-117AD)

A large group of 845 sherds of pottery from the primary fill (1219) of the recut [1251] of the substantial ditch in the access road was of Flavian or Flavian-Trajanic type. A further group of 78 sherds

Code	Description	Source
BB1	Black burnished ware. Black fabric with abundant, medium subangular quartz. (Tomber and Dore 1998 BB1 DOR)	Dorset BB1
CC	Colour-coat ware. Fine white ware with orange-brown colour coat. Sparse medium quartz and orange inclusions	Nene Valley or South Carlton, Lincoln
CT	Vesicular ware. Grey-brown fabric with irregular ill-sorted vesicles	
CTA2	Dales ware. Shell-tempered ware, brown with reddish-brown margins. (Tomber and Dore 1998 DAL SH)	N Lincs/ Yorkshire
CTB	Shell-tempered ware. Brown shell-tempered ware, without margins of Dales ware. Thicker bodies than Dales ware	
DBY	Derbyshire ware. (Tomber and Dore 1998 DER CO)	Belper area
DR20	Dressel 20 oil amphora. (Tomber and Dore 1998 BAT AM)	South Spain
EYCT	Late East Yorkshire calcite gritted ware. East Yorkshire calcite-gritted ware. (Tomber and Dore 1998 HUNT CG)	East Yorkshire
FLA	White ware. Mostly with moderate medium subangular quartz and sparse. Medium, rounded orange/brown inclusions but one inclusion-free sherd	Local
GLAZED	Glazed ware. Oxidised ware with ?clear or yellowish brown glaze	Possibly south England
GRB	Grey ware, indeterminate quartz tempered	
GRB1	Early grey ware. Grey ware with pale, sometimes almost white core and moderate, medium, subangular quartz, sparse red and brown or black medium rounded inclusions	Local
GRC	Gritty grey ware. Hard grey ware with abundant, coarse, angular and subangular quartz	Yorkshire – known at Catterick, Piercebridge, kilns at Green Hammerton
H2	Handmade grit-tempered ware	
MH	Mancetter-Hartshill mortarium. (Tomber and Dore 1998 WH MAH)	Near Coventry
MW	Early white ware mortarium. White/cream ware with moderate, medium, subangular quartz	Local
NV	Nene Valley colour-coated ware. (Tomber and Dore 1998 LNV CC)	Nene Valley near Peterborough
OAB1	Early oxidised ware. Oxidised ware with moderate, medium, subangular quartz and sparse medium rounded orange/brown inclusions	Local
PRIA	Handmade pre-Roman Iron Age ware.	
RBB1	Rossington Black burnished ware 1. (Tomber and Dore 1998 ROS BB1)	Rossington Bridge, Doncaster
SYGRB	South Yorkshire grey ware. Medium grey ware with abundant medium subrounded and subangular quartz	Kilns around Doncaster or local kilns working in same tradition
SYGRB6	South Yorkshire grey ware, hard. Very hard, medium grey ware with abundant medium subrounded and subangular quartz	Kilns around Doncaster or local kilns working in same tradition
SYM	South Yorkshire mortarium. (Tomber and Dore 1998 CANT WS)	Cantley/South Yorkshire kilns around Doncaster.
SYOAB	South Yorkshire oxidised ware. Medium oxidised ware with abundant medium subrounded and subangular quartz	Kilns around Doncaster
TS	Samian	Samian workshops
UNK	Indeterminate	

Table 2. List of pottery ware codes

from a near complete honey pot of the same date range came from (1586), the fill of pit [1587] in the northern part of the car park. Smaller groups of this type of pottery also came from the fills of posthole [1132], pits [1140] and [1585] in the north part of the car park and ditch terminus [1623] in the access road. The fabrics in this phase were easily recognised even in undiagnostic bodysherds and a further 21 contexts were assigned to this phase although these could be later in date since they contained only a handful of sherds each.

The wares present comprised grey wares, GRB1, with a light grey or white-grey core, white wares and pink wares, FLA1 and 2, white mortarium ware, oxidised wares, OAB1, and one glazed beaker (Figures 16-17). The fabrics are very similar to one another apart from colour and appeared to be the same basic clay. Some vessels were burnt or misfired and some sherds seemed very soft, possibly underfired. The grey ware with white core has been identified at Doncaster and Templeborough previously by the author in forms of Flavian-Trajanic

Ware	Nos	Weight	Rim %	Rel % nos	Rel % weight	Rel % EVES
BB1	92	788.9	115	4.5	2.7	4.6
Colour-coat	5	6.8	5	0.2	0.0	0.2
Dales ware	20	118.6	18	1.0	0.4	0.7
Derbyshire ware	1	7.5		0.0	0.0	0.0
Dressel 20 oil amphora	1	68.9		0.0	0.2	0.0
Early grey ware	708	6296	803	34.7	21.3	31.9
Early oxidised ware	206	1938.1	168	10.1	6.6	6.7
Early white ware mortarium	17	1156.2	61	0.8	3.9	2.4
Glazed ware	2	6	10	0.1	0.0	0.4
Grey misfired mortarium	1	64.2		0.0	0.2	0.0
Grey ware	12	101.5	20	0.6	0.3	0.8
Gritty grey ware	4	86	13	0.2	0.3	0.5
Handmade grit-tempered ware	18	210.9	27	0.9	0.7	1.1
Handmade PRIA	5	16.9		0.2	0.1	0.0
Indeterminate	1	9.7		0.0	0.0	0.0
Late East Yorkshire calcite gritted ware	6	67.3	6	0.3	0.2	0.2
Mancetter-Hartshill mortarium	4	198	7	0.2	0.7	0.3
Mancetter-Hartshill type mortarium	8	164.4	11	0.4	0.6	0.4
Nene Valley colour-coated ware	2	50.5		0.1	0.2	0.0
Rossington BB1	30	423.1	94	1.5	1.4	3.7
S Yorks grey ware	607	14688.5	765	29.7	49.7	30.4
S Yorks grey ware, hard	3	35.1		0.1	0.1	0.0
S Yorks oxidised ware	18	167.2		0.9	0.6	0.0
S Yorkshire mortarium	10	172.6	39	0.5	0.6	1.6
Shell-t ware	1	2.9		0.0	0.0	0.0
Vesicular ware	19	80.5	22	0.9	0.3	0.9
White ware	205	2346.5	287	10.0	7.9	11.4
Samian	36	307	43	1.8	1.0	1.7
Total	2042	29579.8	2514	100	100	100

Table 3. Quantities of wares

type – reeded rim bowls, rusticated jars etc. In addition to this group two vessels in SYGRB were present. One of these was a neckless everted rim jar with stabbing along the shoulder (no. 26) and the other is a bead rim deep bowl (no. 21). These have the abundant subrounded quartz typical of grey wares from the Doncaster kiln group. The neckless jar came from (1054), a fill of the east-west ditch [1010/1018/1024/1055/1057], and was associated with other late first-early second century types while the sherds from a deep bead rim bowl came from (1219). Given the large number of early types from (1219), it would seem likely that the two abraded rim sherds from this bowl are intrusive.

A range of Flavian-Trajanic types were made in these wares. Bowls were predominantly reeded rim types (nos 10-11), most in fabric GRB1 with insloping rims and the outermost reed often prominent, a

smaller number in GRB1, OAB1 or FLA1 with flat reeded rims. A carinated cordoned bodysherd came from a GRB1 bowl developed from the late La Tene cordoned carinated bowl series (no.14) and a campanulate GRB1 bowl with everted rim seems to be based on the TN campanulate bowl series (no. 12, Greene 1978, Figure 46) and was popular in Britain in the Flavian period. This form did continue to be made into the later second century in Yorkshire (Bell and Evans 2002 type B11.1) and elsewhere in the North but the fabric of this vessel compares closely with that of the other Flavian –Trajanic grey wares – rusticated jars and reeded-rim bowls, so an early date is consistent with this. A GRB1 flanged sherd from a bowl with horizontal flange (no. 13) may be copying the earlier samian forms as Ritterling 12 (pre-AD80) and the earlier Curle 11s (Flavian). A significant number of fine white ware bowls were present. These included hemispherical bowls with a bead rim and cordon defining a plain upper zone (no. 18, Rush 2000, Figure 49 no.123 in Flavian phase). No decoration on the main part of the bowl was found. Another bowl form had a moulded rim with two or three external grooves resulting in a cordoned effect (nos 16-7 and 24). The inside of this rim was sometimes slightly dished and the lower body was carinated with cordons/grooves on the carination. These may belong to the campanulate bowl form also present at Malton (Swan 2002, Figure 4 no. 38) for which Swan suggests a relationship with samian form 29. A similar form was present at the Flavian-Trajanic kilns at Derby Racecourse (Brassington 1971 no. 23 and 1980 nos 523-24) and at Castleford in fort phase 1 (Rush 2000, Figure 9 nos 116-21). At Colchester a similar form often has handles and has a Continental derivation, with a date range from the Claudio-Neronian to late first or early second century suggested (Symonds and Wade 1999 type 326/331, Figure 6.7 nos. 173-8). In London, Marsh found a similar group of vessels were common in the late first century (1978 type 44) and traces influences in their form from samian ware, North African slip ware and Terra Nigra forms. Dishes were uncommon but FLA basal sherds from a platter with a kicked base (no. 28) and another with a concentric cordon inside the base are also of early date, belonging to this phase.

The everted rim jars (nos 1-2) are often rusticated with linear or web rustication (no. 2). The other jar form was the necked jars with short everted rims and hooked rims (nos 3-6). The numbers of necked jars might argue for an earlier date in the Flavian-Trajanic period if compared with the ratio found in a Flavian group at Middlewich (Leary 2008, 72) and this type disappears completely by phase 3 at Nostell. One basal sherd from a flat based vessel was pierced with small holes, pre-firing, forming a strainer or colander (no. 34) of some sort. Ring and dot beakers (Greene 1978) were made both in grey ware with applied ring and dots and in white ware with orange brown painted rings and dots (no. 7). White and pinkish white ware flagons with fairly upright ringed necks (nos 9 and 23) and honeypots (nos 8 and 22) also belong to this phase. The honeypots had rather triangular rims with flat tops (at Colchester, Symonds and Wade 1999, Figure 6.10 nos 250-1 type 175, dated Claudio-Neronian (41-68

AD) to late first century). Lids had simple flat or slightly beaded rim tips (nos 20, 25, 27 and 30).

The mortaria in a cream to yellow ware, with inclusions similar to the other early wares, was submitted to Kay Hartley and were found to be of special interest. Notably, a substantial proportion were made in hitherto unknown fabric and bore characteristics indicative of a nearby mortarium production site (see Hartley, this volume).

Two sherds were sent to David Williams for comment – an unusual rim sherd of a large flagon or small amphora type (no. 55) and a thick body sherd also of amphora type. He commented that it is possible that this distinctive rim with double moulded neck could be from the first century AD wine amphora Gauloise 3, or perhaps a variation on that form (cf. Laubenheimer in Williams and Keay 2006) although it is difficult to be certain and the thick bodysherd came from near to the base of an amphora. The rim sherd is creamy buff-beige in colour and hard fired, while the slightly gritty fabric suggests a source outside of the main production area of *Gallia Narbonensis* (Laubenheimer in Williams and Keay 2006). The thick bodysherd was similar in fabric to the rim and so it is possible that they may well have come from the same vessel. Such amphorae are rare in Britain although a group were identified "in a range of fabric variations" in 1st century contexts in London (Davies, Richardson and Tomber 1994, 18 and Figure 12). Given the similarity in fabric between the rim and bodysherds from (1219) and the other coarse wares including the mortaria, it is possible that the vessel is produced more locally than France and a regional copy would seem much more likely than an actual French vessel. The manufacture of a first century Gallic amphora type 3, uncommon in Roman Britain, is somewhat unexpected and perhaps implies a soldier/potter who had recently come from working in that region. A further basal sherd from (1219) with footring base may also belong to an amphora of this type since it seemed rather large for a flagon form.

Symonds cited manufacture of Gallic amphora types in London, Verulamium (St Albans), Hoo in Kent and Alice Holt with further instances of amphorae in local fabrics at Colchester, Usk, the Nene Valley, Caistor-by-Norwich, Mancetter-Hartshill and Brampton. He also cites possible examples of locally produced amphorae at Watercrook, Lancaster, Ribchester, Birrens, Biglands, Malton, Cramond and Camelon but qualifies these northern instances with the rider that they may not be large enough to be considered true amphora (Symonds 2003, 57-8). Pertinent to the vessel at Nostell, Rush identified several large flagons or amphorae of this type in local wares at Castleford from the Flavian phases of the fort and *vicus* (2000, Figure 43 no. 6 and Figure 54 no. 184). A further two vessels listed as "lagena" from Doncaster High Street and town centre may be similar instances (Buckland and Magilton 1986, Figure 49 no. 303 and Figure 41 no. 304) although without specialist identification or fabric analysis a source in Gaul cannot be ruled out. At a later date at York, Swan and McBride identified a form made in Ebor ware as an "amphorette" (2002 type E) and dates it to the third century Ebor potteries. Parallels are drawn with similar vessels at Soller in the Rhineland (Swan and McBride 2002, 218) and a function holding wine decanted from barrels suggested. Such a function would be attractive for the Nostell vessel also.

Thus although unusual, evidence for British made amphora or amphora-type vessels is present certainly around London and the south east with evidence extending at least as far as the Midlands and York itself. Whether these vessels functioned in the same way as the Gallic examples, for long distance transportation of wine, is far from clear. The presence of a Gallic amphora potter, C ALBVCI, in London, stamping local SLOW amphorae (Symonds 2003, 55) implies that at least in London the vessels produced were of the same type and function. Away from London details are more tenuous, petrological analysis is needed to source the vessels and details such as stamps, perhaps pitch linings and full profiles would do much to clarify the classification and function of these amphora-like vessels.

As regards the dating of the assemblage from (1219), although many of the common forms in this phase have a date range through the late first and early second century, several types are most common in the late first century suggesting a Flavian date range (69-96AD). The amphora, honey pots, necked everted and hooked rim jars, the ring and dot beakers, the moulded rim bowls

and the flagons all point towards late first century date and the forms are well paralleled at Castleford particularly in the fort phase 1 group dated to AD71/4-86. The early samian is all mid to late first century in date including sherds from four vessels dated to AD 40-80, 40-100, 50-100 and 60-100 and although only one of these was stratified in a phase 2 context, they must derive from this phase (see Monteil, this volume).

All the grey, oxidised and white wares in this phase appeared to be made using the same basic clay. In context (1219) several misfired or burnt sherds revealed this quite clearly with vessels partially fired grey, orange and white showing clearly that these used the same basic clay but were fired to the desired colours as required. Such a concentration of vessels in a single basic fabric is most unusual and may indicate production in the neighbourhood. The style of vessels implies military related potters and at this time in this region, native rural settlements were not acquiring this quantity or range of fully Romanised pots and were still using ceramics of the pre-Roman Iron Age tradition. Together with the assemblage of mortaria (Hartley, this volume), which also show evidence for local, military-related production, the character of the assemblage indicates the nearby presence of a potter working in a wholly Roman tradition with strong Continental links with Gaul and, as such, the potter's association with the military is certain.

In addition to this "local" group one grey ware jar with a short everted rim and a row of stabs on the shoulder above a groove (no. 26) was in a fabric unlike the other grey ware used in this phase - GRB1. The jar was in a dark grey ware with moderate rather rounded quartz similar to the later South Yorkshire grey wares. The form is more likely to be Flavian-Trajanic and the fabric is not unlike that used for the earlier Doncaster products for which kilns have not yet been excavated (Swan 2002, Figure 12 no. 148-50). One rusticated jar with a short everted rim from pit [1603], the earlier of the two rectangular clay-lined pits or cisterns, was also in South Yorkshire grey ware. Rusticated ware seems to have been made as late as the mid-second century at the Doncaster kilns but the later examples have a distinctive recurved rim unlike this example. As with the aforementioned stabbed jar, this vessel should belong to the late first to early second century production at Doncaster.

The glazed beaker (no. 33) is a small version of the neckless everted rim jars made in grey and white ware. The fabric is unlike that made at centres such as Derby Little Chester but is not unlike Southern British Glazed ware (Tomber and Dore 1998, 213) dated from c.80AD to as late as the Hadrianic period.

Phase 3: Mid-late second century

Phase 3 groups were characterised by the presence of BB1 or Yorkshire grey ware copies of BB1 types and the decline in numbers of the phase 2 wares. One BB1 jar with wavy line neck burnish from pit [1034], no. 35, part of the pit group in the southwest part of the car park, dates to before the mid-second century when this motif declined in popularity. The form of this vessel pointed to a Hadrianic date (117-138 AD). The near complete rusticated jar in SYGRB (no. 44) from clay-lined pit [1603] mentioned under phase 2 may be of this date rather than Trajanic (98-117 AD). Many of the second century vessels could be dated to the mid-late second century and these were made up largely of South Yorkshire grey and black burnished wares of this date. Forms in BB1 or copying BB1 included neckless jars with short everted rims and acute lattice burnish (no. 43), flat rim bowls/dishes, plain- and grooved rim dishes (as no. 46, Gillam 1976 nos 31, 68-9, 76 and 79), South Yorkshire lipped bowls/dishes (no. 36), everted-rim jars (no. 38), large everted-rim jars (no. 39), bead-rim deep bowls (no. 37 and as no. 51) and shouldered wide-mouthed jars (Buckland et al. 1980 types Ca, Cb, Ea, F, Hb and Hc-d). Sherds from one colour-coated roughcast beaker, indented, were in a fine white ware with orange brown colour coat. This vessel may be from the South Carlton kilns at Lincoln dating from the mid to late second century, or Nene Valley kilns, and seemed too coarse for Cologne. A small number of samian sherds gave a similar date range to the coarse wares. In this phase the fabrics found in phase 2 are only present as residual sherds and there appears to be a complete change in the source of the pottery as well as the types being used. It is possible that there was a hiatus in occupation in the early second century.

The largest group, over 100 sherds, came from the backfill of the later clay-lined pit/cistern [1168] and included much of a flat rim SYGRB bowl of the second century (no. 36). In pit [1401], to the north side of the main car park excavation, most of a mid-to late second century Rossington BB1 jar (no. 43) and a flat rim bowl was present through the fills. A samian bowl form 37, dating to 125-145 AD, was also present in this pit scattered through the fills in the same way as the BB jar. The SYGRB rusticated jar from the earlier clay-lined pit/cistern [1603] was also substantially present (though fragmented) and much of a bead rim dish in SYGRB (no. 41) came from fill (1263) in the corn-drier [1265]. Buckland et al (1980 type B) record these dishes as being present in the South Yorkshire kilns from the mid-second to the mid-fourth century although numbers decline after the third century. A near complete handled jar from the evaluation phase of excavation in context (306) is of South Yorkshire type but has a long date range from the mid-second to the mid fourth century (Plate 16). The hard fabric compares best with the Cantley products suggesting a late second to third century date range. These near complete but fragmented vessels may be disturbed structured deposits of some kind but their abraded and fragmented condition makes firm interpretation difficult.

Plate 16. Near complete handled jar from evaluation context (306) in the process of excavation

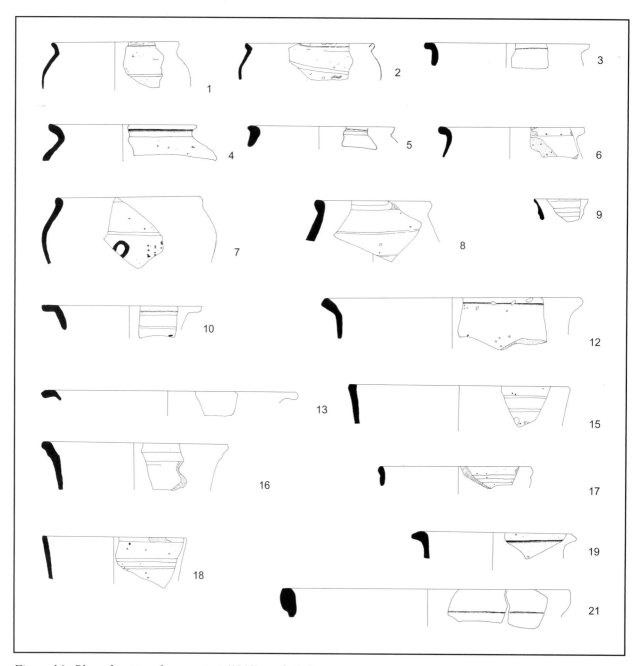

Figure 16. Phase 2 pottery from context (1219), scale 1:4
See below for catalogue

Catalogue of illustrated phase 2 sherds from context (1219) (Figure 16)

1. GRB1 neckless jar with short everted rim. Single groove on shoulder.

2. GRB1 neckless jar with short everted rim and rustication.

3. GRB1 jar with sloping neck and short everted rim tip. Appears to be distorted.

4. GRB1 necked jar with short everted rim tip.

5. GRB1 necked jar with short everted rim tip.

6. GRB1 necked jar with hooked rim.

7. FLA1 neckless jar/beaker with brown painted ring and dot panels below a shoulder groove. Some of the sherds are grey.

8. GRB1/FLA1 honey pot type jar with triangular flat rim and groove outside upper body. A small rise near the break suggests a handle joined adjacent to the groove. This vessel had grey surfaces in places and it was difficult to know which firing effect was intended.

9. FLA1 ring necked flagon with angular rings and fairly upright neck.

10. GRB1 bowl with flat reeded rim.

11. GRB1 carinated bowl with reeded rim with pronounced outer reed, higher than the others. (NOT ILLUSTRATED)

12. GRB1 everted-rim bowl, perhaps a campanulate form.

13. GRB1 flange, probably from flanged bowl.

14. OAB/GRB carinated bowl with concave upper body and central groove. Soft fired with some traces of a grey surface so this may be a grey ware. (NOT ILLUSTRATED)

15. OAB1 upright flat rim with multiple grooves below.

16. FLA1 bowl with double moulded rim.

17. FLA1 carinated bowl with double moulded rim.

18. FLA1 bowl with bead rim above plain zone then double groove.

19. FLA1 flanged rim with groove near wall junction, probably a bowl.

20. GRB1 lid with rim tip grooved on both sides. (NOT ILLUSTRATED)

21. SYGRB squared sectioned rim of wide-mouthed vessel, probably a deep bowl form.

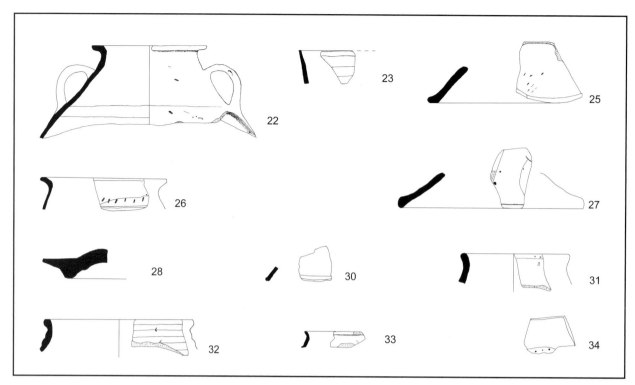

Figure 17. Phase 2 pottery from other contexts, scale 1:4
See below for catalogue

Catalogue of illustrated phase 2 sherds from other contexts (Figure 17)

22. OAB1 pale orange with creamy surfaces. Honey pot with flat everted rim and double ribbed handles on shoulder to neck. Much of vessel is present but no base. Phase 2 (1586)

23. OAB1 ring neck flagon with upright rim. Phase 3 (1000)

24. FLA1 bowl with moulded rim. Phase 2 (1054) (NOT ILLUSTRATED)

25. GRB1 lid. Phase 2 (1054)

26. SYGRB black surfaced neckless jar with short everted rim, shoulder groove with stabbed decoration above groove. Phase 2 (1054)

27. GRB1 lid. Phase 2 (1056)

28. FLA/GRB1 footring base from dish or platter with basal kick. Another sherd from this or another vessel of the same type was present in phase 2 group (1219). Phase 4 (1069).

29. GRB/FLA1 white with greyish tinge to surfaces, closed vessel with grooved wavy line decoration. Phase 2 (1139) (NOT ILLUSTRATED)

30. OAB1 plain lid. Phase 2 (1139)

31. OAB1CC narrow necked jar rim. Phase 2 (1154)

32. GRB1 jar with multiple cordoned body and triangular rim. Phase 4 pit fill (1261)

33. GLZ glazed everted rim beaker Phase 2 (1266)

34. GRB1 base with pre-firing perforation, strainer. Phase 2 (1622).

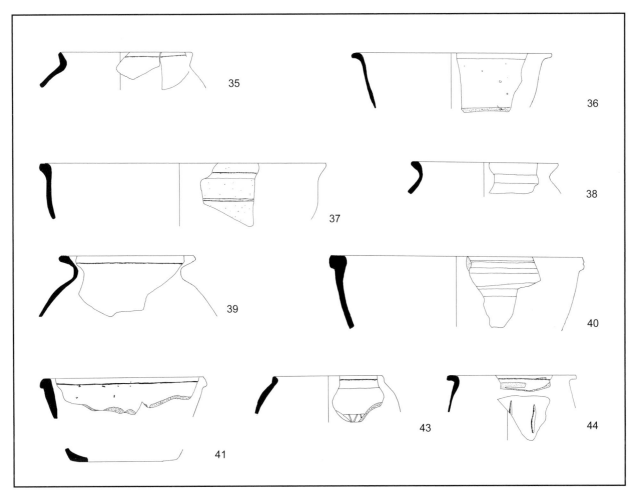

Figure 18. Phase 3 pottery, scale 1:4
See below for catalogue

Catalogue of illustrated phase 3 sherds (Figure 18)

35. BB1 jar with upright neck (Gillam 1976 no. 2) early-mid second century. Faint traces of wavy line burnish on neck, a motif that declined by the mid-second century. (1033)

36. SYGRB flat rim bowl. Mid to late second century. (1167)

37. SYGRB bead rim deep bowl with grooved shoulder. (1167)

38. SYGRB everted rim jar with off set shoulder as those made at Doncaster potteries. (1167)

39. SYGRB narrow mouthed vessel with everted rim, perhaps a lugged jar type. (1167)

40. SYGRB bifid rim deep bowl (Buckland et al 1980 type Hc-d) restricted to second century. (1262)

41. SYGRB 10 sherds from the rim, body and base of a bead-rim dish. (1263)

43. RBB1 neckless everted rim jar with acute lattice burnish (Gillam 1976 no 31) mid-to late second century. (1413)

44. Most of a SYGRB neckless everted rim rusticated jar, linear rustication. (1601)

In corn-drier [1265] the rest of the pottery from fills (1262) and (1261) suggested this feature was being used during the second half of the second century and fell out of use by the third century. The pottery from deposit (1262) included sherds from a BB1 flat rim bowl or dish of second century date, several SYGRB sherds including the rim of a bifid (i.e. split in two) rim deep bowl (no. 40), a type which Buckland et al (1980 type Hc-d) noted was limited to the second century kilns and a small bead rim deep bowl. These types date from the mid-second century onwards with some types in decline before the end of that century, so a mid- to late second century date is indicated. The infill deposit (1261) was dated by sherds from late BB1 jars with splayed rims to the third century at the earliest but much of the pottery was redeposited phase 2 type with rusticated jar sherds, reeded rim bowls, a jar with multiple cordons and a short everted rim in GRB1, as well as an SYGRB bead rim deep bowl of the mid-second century or later. The samian from (1261) dated to the second half of the second century (145-180, 150-200 and 120-200 AD) (Monteil, this volume).

Posthole [1635], near the corn-drier, contained more sherds of similar date including BB1 and SYGRB sherds including sherds from a grooved-rim dish probably of mid- second century type (Gillam 1976 nos 68-9). In pit [1124] in the centre of the main car park excavation 30 sherds included fragments from a RBB1 plain-rim dish (Gillam 1976 no. 76) and jars with acute lattice burnish of the mid to late second century.

The other features in this phase contained small numbers of sherds, less than eleven, of the types mentioned above. These can only be given a ter-minus post quem in this phase as they contain only undiagnostic sherds of the second century or later.

Phase 4: The third century

This phase is primarily defined by the presence of later types particularly third century BB1 jars with splayed rims and obtuse lattice burnish (Gillam 1976 nos 10-12), Dales ware, hammerhead and reeded rim mortaria from Mancetter-Hartshill and South Yorkshire forms such as the cupped rim jar (no. 47), Buckland et al 1980 Eb), which is common in the third century. Most of the groups

were small except secondary ditch fill (1069) of ditch [1071/1085/1100/1195]. This contained some 166 sherds which included BB1 jars with splayed rims (no. 45), South Yorkshire grey ware deep bowls (nos 48) and everted rim jars as well as sherds from an early mortarium. (These must have been residual as the ditch is dated to phase 5 on stratigraphic grounds.) The late fill group from corn-drier [1265] is discussed above and although it contained late BB1 jar rims these may have arrived late in the silting up of this feature. Sherds from a Mancetter-Hartshill reeded rim hammer-head mortarium came from pits [1032] and [1036], in the southwest part of the car park, and dated to c.AD240-300. A South Yorkshire wall-sided mor-tarium from L-shaped entrance ditch [1119] dates to the third to fourth century, probably from the mid-third to fourth century and a South Yorkshire smooth hammerhead mortarium from another pit in the southwest of the car park [1095] is probably of third century type. Sherds from a BB1 splayed rim jar of mid- to late third century or later type and two SYGRB1 deep bowls (no. 49) were also present in [1119]. The other groups were small but assigned to this phase on the basis of the presence of late BB1 types with splayed rims or obtuse lattice or Dales ware sherds.

Phase 5: Late third to fourth century

Few types of fourth century date were present. Types used as markers for this phase included the developed flanged bowls of the late third to fourth century (no. 50, Buckland et al 1980 type Cc), a late grey gritty ware used to make Dales type jars in the late third to fourth century (no. 53, Bidwell and Croom 2010, Figure 4.4 nos 25a, c and d) and reeded hammerhead mortaria and wall-sided mor-taria with slag trituration grits from the South York-shire kilns. The latest sherd was a pre-Huntcliff jar rim of the early to mid-fourth century (no. 52, Bell and Evans 2002 type J9.1). Pre-Huntcliff types came from late fill (1156) in the probable well [1160] and a calcite gritted basal sherd from fill (1432) of posthole [1433[may also be of this date. A basal sherd from Nene Valley colour-coated bowl of late third or fourth century date came from fill (1038) of pit [1039] in the southwest corner of the car park, sherds from a reeded rim mortarium in a Mancetter type of late third to early fourth

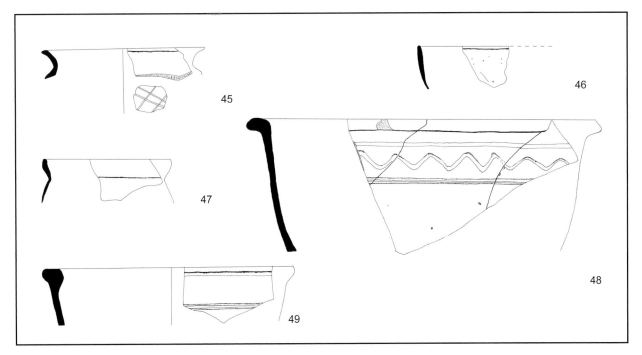

Figure 19. Phase 4 pottery, scale 1:4
See below for catalogue

Catalogue of illustrated phase 4 sherds (Figure 19)

45. BB1 jar with splayed rim, third century or later. A non-adjoining bodysherd had obtuse lattice burnish. (1069)

46. BB1 plain rim dish with intersecting burnished lines (Gillam 1976 no. 79) early third century. (1069)

47. SYGRB cupped rim from jar. (1069)

48. SYGRB much of deep bowl with flat rim and grooved wavy line decoration on upper body. (1083)

49. SYGRB 13 sherds from a small deep bowl with bead rim and double groove outside shoulder. (1117)

---

century date were present in late fill (1098) in ditch [1100] with a developed flanged bowl of the same date. Sherds from a similar mortarium came from secondary fill (1028) of pit [1030]. The fabric of these mortarium sherds has not been previously recorded in association with mortarium types typical for Mancetter-Hartshill. They were certainly made by potters who had learnt their trade there but the fabric suggests that they had moved elsewhere and were active in a small workshop somewhere well to the north probably further north than Doncaster (Hartley, this volume). Sherds from a GRC Dales type jar came from ditch terminus [1189] and a sherd from a developed flanged bowl was present in pit [1218].

Function and site status

The ceramics can give us an indication of the function of a feature or area and of the status of the settlements they represent (Evans 1993 and 2001a). Aspects of status have been explored by examining the wares and vessel types found on different settlement types. Forts and urban settlements tend to have more imports and traded wares and use more fully Roman vessels such as flagons, beakers, cups and bowls and dishes for serving food at table in the Roman way. Rural settlements can lack these traded goods completely and use very few tablewares, the majority of vessels beings jars, not unlike the situation during the pre-Roman Iron Age. At Nostell Priory the different ceramic groups were examined for evidence of this sort.

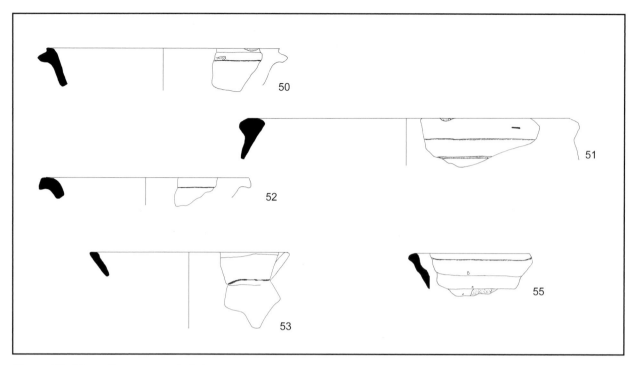

Figure 20. Phase 5 pottery, scale 1:4
See below for catalogue

Catalogue of illustrated phase 5 sherds (Figure 20)

50. SY GRB developed flanged bowl, late third to fourth century. (1098)

51. SY GRB bead rim deep bowl. (1156)

52. EYCT pre-Huntcliff type jar with hooked rim but no internal lid seating. (1156)

53. GRC1 gritty grey ware lid seated jar of Dales type. (1188)

55. FLA amphora rim of Gauloise type 3. (1219)

Phase 2: Flavian-Trajanic period (69-117AD)

This group stood out immediately from assemblages of this date from other rural settlements in West and South Yorkshire with rather more bowl and dishes, despite the lack of samian. The abundance of Roman wares and vessel types was remarkable and contrasted with the usual first or early second century pottery groups from rural settlement in this region, which are characterised by very low levels of Roman pottery and small amounts of hand-made jars in the pre-Roman Iron Age tradition. At Nostell Priory the forms – an amphora, flagons, beakers, "honey pots", white ware bowls and painted beakers – are all typical of military sites of this date. The range of jars (rusticated and grooved shoulder jars) and bowls (reeded rim bowls with fine bowls influenced by samian and Continental military types) would be most unusual for a rural

settlement even in the early second century. The amount of traded wares, such as samian, was low but nonetheless significant at this early date. The group from (1219) included many rather softly fired vessels and partially oxidised/reduced vessels raising the possibility that these were kiln wasters. One or two sherds were distorted although these could be seconds. Fired clay fragments seen during the assessment could belong to a kiln but no conclusive evidence was identified. Surface cracking on some vessels lent weight to the possibility that this is a kiln discard group although, until a kiln is located, this remains speculative. It is unlikely that even the settling of a veteran at Nostell Priory would adequately explain this cache of fine Roman wares. The quantity and range of vessels implies a military related site, perhaps a fort, annexe, *vicus* or an industrial complex. Table 4 demonstrates the

Vessel	Phase 1 (PRIA)	Phase 2	Phase 3	Phase 4	Phase 5	Unphased	Total rim %
Bowl		211	50	14	15		290
TS bowl			13.5	1			14.5
TS dec bowl			17.5				17.5
Dish			77	21			98
TS dish		6				5	11
Bowl/dish				2			2
Beaker			5		20		25
Flagon		60	10				70
Honey pot		115					115
Jar	49	676	224	283	42		1274
Narrow-n jar		24	25	11	20		80
Wide-m bowl		9	62	140	12		223
Wide-m jar			22	92			114
Lid		28		4			32
Mortarium		41		66	11		118
Indeterminate		25			5		30
Total	49	1195	506	634	125	5	2514

Table 4. Rim percentage values for vessel types by phase

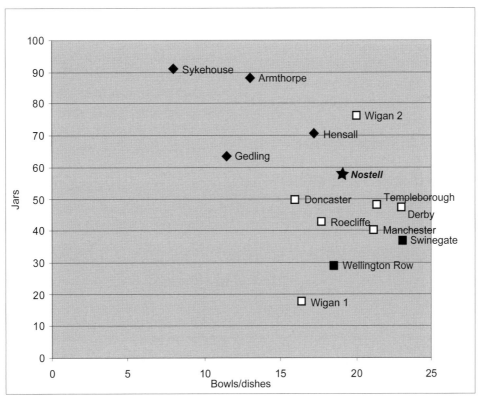

Figure 21. Relative quantification of vessels by vessel types and ceramic phase using rim percentage values on Flavian-Trajanic sites
White rectangles = forts
Black diamonds = rural settlements
Black rectangles = sites in York
Star = Nostell phase 2

unique concentration of vessel forms (and quantities) in the phase 2 assemblage and Figure 21 compares the bowl/dish to jar ratio during Nostell phase 2 to other known sites.

Phases 3-5

In contrast to phase 2, pottery from phases 3 and 4 was typical of second and third century settlement in this region with no flagons, cups and only one beaker and small numbers of fine wares (samian) as shown by Figure 22. Burnt matter and scorching was present on jars of BB1 and SYGRB as is normal for cooking vessels of this type. One SYGRB everted rim jar had a rather distorted rim but this defect would not have rendered it unusable. The Phase 5 pottery group was too small for this kind of analysis.

Trade

In phase 2 the majority of the pottery appeared to be made in the same fabric, although fired to different colours, and is likely to be of local origin. A single glazed ware beaker (no. 33) is in an orange ware with glaze firing to a rich brown colour where present over the clay body. This may have belonged to a soldier coming from southern England rather than representing trade. The samian came from Gaul. The Spanish oil amphora could belong to phases 2, 3 or 4 in date.

In phase 3 the local wares of phase 2 were completely replaced by a coarser ware, mainly types characteristic of the South Yorkshire kilns. It is possible that nearer kilns in West Yorkshire were also making these forms but the fabrics cannot be readily differentiated and no kilns have been excavated. Rossington Bridge BB1 was identified but the group may also include some Dorset BB1. One sherd of Derbyshire ware was present. This jar may have been traded on account of its contents and these jars have also been found at Hemsworth (Leary 2009). Derbyshire ware appeared in the mid-second century at Derby Little Chester but was absent in a mid-fourth century group in Derbyshire (Birss 1985, table 5 and Birss 1986). Derbyshire ware does occur in small quantities at Gunhills, Armthorpe (less than 1%, Leary 2008) and Edlington Wood (Phillips 1973) but otherwise these wares are absent on rural settlements. Derbyshire ware did however occur in small quantities at urban and military sites in Yorkshire such as Doncaster (Buckland and Magilton 1986, 175 no. 169), Templeborough, Ilkley and Slack (Gillam 1940) and at villa sites such as Stancil (Whiting 1943, 267), predominantly in second century contexts where dated.

In phase 4 South Yorkshire grey wares continued to dominate the assemblage with Dorset BB1 jars and dishes and some Dales ware. At Castleford Rush

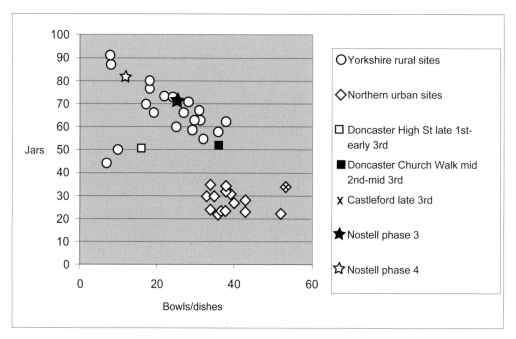

Figure 22. Relative proportions of jars to bowls/dishes on west and south Yorkshire rural sites, northern military sites, urban sites and Nostell Priory phases 3 and 4

noted a sharp decline in the supply of BB1 by the beginning of the fourth century and a rise in Dales ware, and East Yorkshire grey and calcite gritted wares (2000, 158). Mancetter-Hartshill mortaria from near Coventry and mortaria from the South Yorkshire kilns (Annable 1960) were present. A very small amount of Nene Valley colour coated ware was identified from near Peterborough (Perrin 1999).

In phase 5, from the late third to early fourth century, the South Yorkshire grey ware contribution dropped dramatically from over 80% to a mere 27%. This shortfall was made up with smaller amounts of gritty grey ware Dales type jars, BB1 jars, Pre-Huntcliff ware, more traded mortaria from Mancetter-Hartshill and Cantley and fine wares from the Nene Valley industry. This appears to mark the decline of the South Yorkshire potteries and a similar decline was noted at site C4SA on the Darrington to Dishforth road scheme (Leary 2007, 251). In this phase two mortaria sherds, from (1028), the upper fill of pit [1030], and (1098), the fill of late ditch [1100], were similar in form to Mancetter-Hartshill products but were identified by Kay Hartley (this volume) as a local product almost certainly made by potters who had trained at the Mancetter-Hartshill potteries.

3.2 A note on the mortaria

Kay Hartley

Introduction

A mortarium (plural "mortaria") was a class of Roman kitchen vessel, bowl-shaped in form with a flanged rim (adapted for gripping) and a spout. Characteristically grit was usually embedded in its inner surface. They were used for grinding, pounding or mixing foods and are an important indicator of people using romanised food preparation methods. They are a well-catalogued type of pottery with distinctive forms and often include maker's stamps, from which it is possible to trace trade routes and the movement of potters between different workshops. The mortaria recovered from this excavation were identified as unusual and significant and were therefore submitted to Kay Hartley for additional comment.

Quantification

There were 29 sherds weighing 1700gms from an absolute minimum of 14 vessels or an absolute maximum of 18 vessels. Fabric has been examined with a hand lens at x20 magnification. A total of five fabric types (two of which are variants) were identified as shown in the tables below (Tables 5 and 6).

Comments

The mortaria in this small sample of 29 sherds from 14-18 individual vessels show mortarium usage in this area. They indicate the greatest activity in the Flavian or Flavian-Trajanic period (69-96 or 69-117 AD) with a very thin, intermittent, presence in the third century possibly going into the fourth century. So small a number cannot, of course, represent a complete picture of the usage of mortaria throughout the Roman period even in this small area, but they do, however, highlight this area as of quite unusual, even outstanding, interest.

The mortaria of special interest are those in Fabrics 1 (M1-M11) and 2 (M12 and M13) because it is virtually certain that these are local products probably produced in the immediate vicinity. Although absolute proof is not present, it is certainly possible that those in Fabric 1 could be waste products from a nearby kiln. Fabric 2 is a variant of Fabric 1, being produced up to 200 years later. There are 8-11 individual vessels in Fabric 1 and three in Fabric 2.

These two fabrics are previously unknown especially in combination with the rim-profiles and the characteristics of the mortaria concerned. They have enough in common to indicate a common source especially taking into consideration the difference in date of up to 200 years. Those in Fabric 2 are easy to assess because in rim profile they are so typical of Mancetter-Hartshill mortaria forms that they can be readily attributed to one or more potters who had moved from the main potteries in the midlands during the late third or early fourth centuries. Why they chose to go to Nostell is not immediately obvious.

Fabric code	Weight (g)	Sherds	Vessel count	Date range
1 (Local)	1190	15	8-11	70-120 AD
2 (Local)	175	5	3	c. 270-330 AD
3 MH2 (Mancetter-Hartshill)	165	3	1-2	c. 200-260 AD
4 S.Yorks	115	4	1	3rd to 4th century
5 S.Yorks	55	2	1	Late 3rd to 4th century
Total	1700	29	14-18	

Table 5. Quantities of each ware and date range

Context	Number of sherds	Vessels	Mortarium number
Fabric 1: local vicinity (within the period 70-120 AD)			
1001	2	1	M1
1069	2	1	M2
1158	1	0-1	M3
1219	8	4-6	M4, M5, M6, M7, M8, M9
1501	1	1	M10
1622	1	1	M11
TOTAL	15	8-11	
Fabric 2: local vicinity (270-330 AD)			
1028	3	1	M12
1098	1(breaks modern)	1	M13
1335	1	1	M14
TOTAL	5	3	
Fabric 3: Mancetter-Hartshill potteries, Warwickshire (c. 200-260 AD)			
1031/1035	2	1	M15, M16
1156	1	0-1	M17
TOTAL	3	1-2	
Fabric 4: South Yorkshire, ?Cantley (3rd- 4th century)			
1094	4	1	M18
Fabric 5: South Yorkshire, probably Cantley (Late 3rd to 4th century)			
1117	2	1	M19

Table 6. Quantities of each ware by context

The 8-11 mortaria in Fabric 1 provide the largest group in this sample that are datable to a single, limited period. Most of the coarseware together with these mortaria fit better into the Flavian or Flavian-Trajanic period (69-96 or 69-117 AD) than any other. Mortarium rim-profiles generally comparable to these might be dated up to c.120 AD. There are slight differences in this group, for example in the way that the trituration grit was applied: on M3 and M7 it is tiny and packed together whereas on M4 and M9 it is composed of tiny to largish grits randomly distributed. The constituents of the trituration grit, and the inclusions are consistent within the group. These rim-profiles in this fabric cannot be matched in the mortaria made in the big known potteries of the period ie. in the Verulamium region at Brockley Hill, Little Munden or Radlett (Tomber and Dore 1998: 154; Hartley and Tomber 2006, 95-98) or in the Noyonais Group of potteries in the Oise/Somme area of northern France (Hartley and Tomber 2006 22-24; Hartley 1998, 199-203). There is nothing in the sample to suggest that the Nostell mortaria were stamped though there is not enough surviving of any single vessel for certainty.

As a group, they have features that are consistent with production in the immediate vicinity:

a.   M9 is overfired to black and dark grey almost throughout;

b.　　part of the end of the spout of M4 has flaked off at the point where the extra clay had been added to form the spout – always an area of weakness;

c.　　none of the sherds show any positive wear and M3, M4 and M7 which have the best surviving surfaces are positively unworn.

These are features that occur in waste mortaria; they are not individually proof of production, but added together they provide convincing circumstantial evidence. This is backed up by the complete absence of even the smallest body sherd from either of the major producers of the period whose products were ubiquitous throughout Roman Britain. Also there is no known source from which they are likely to have come.

This group of mortaria are the earliest on the site, they form a tight group in fabric and a close enough group in profile. They were not imported to the site from any known pottery in Britain or even on the Continent. The only conclusion possible is that they are from a workshop in the vicinity. There is no lack of suitable clay from the Coal Measures in West Yorkshire and adjacent areas: mortaria were made at Aldborough and Castleford in the Roman period and white and light buff firing clays were used in the earlier medieval period (pers. comm. C. Cumberpatch) and in more recent times in making the Leeds pottery.

If local production is accepted this raises further questions. Nostell was fairly certainly in an area where the ordinary population were still living in a late Iron Age tradition that did not include mortaria or wheelmade pottery. No potter or potters making Romano-British type wheelmade pottery would set up a workshop at Nostell without having a market sympathetic to their products. There is only one obvious reason why it would happen and that would be in order to service a military establishment. Castleford would be the nearest known fort or fortress and a mortarium fragment from there (Rush et al 2000, Figure 93, no.69) appears to be similar to M6, but nothing which is published matches the rest of the Nostell mortaria. One could certainly expect some of the mortaria made at Nostell to reach Castleford, but it is probably too far away to be the intended 'market' for the pottery made in the vicinity of Nostell. It seems more likely

that the Nostell pottery was made for an unlocated fort. Obviously only further investigation of the area can clarify this very interesting situation, but the fact that the mortaria are not easily paralleled in England could mean that the potters and the military unit came direct from the Continent rather than elsewhere in Britain.

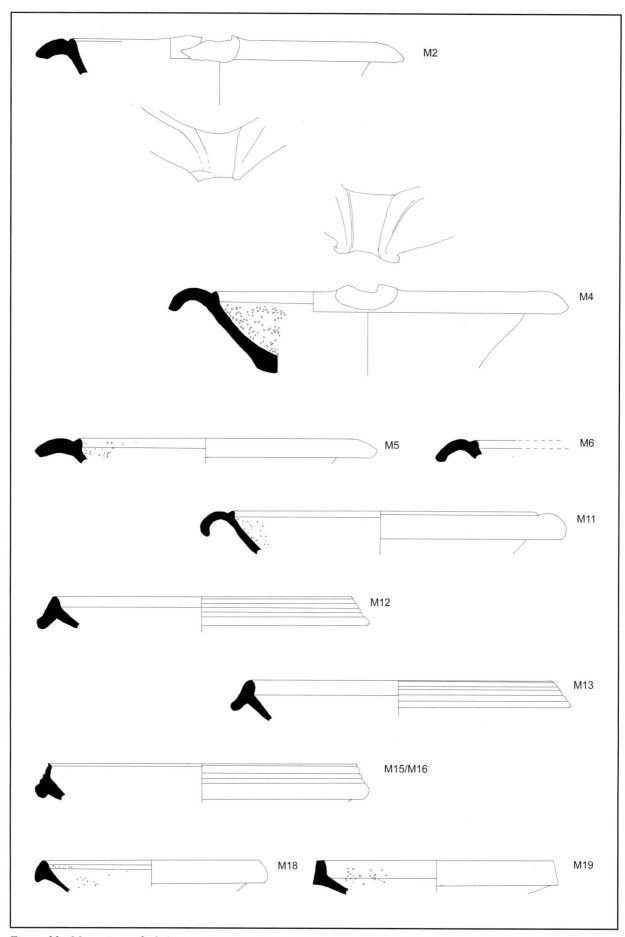

Figure 23. Mortaria, scale 1:4
See below for catalogue

Catalogue of illustrated mortaria sherds (Figure 23)

Fabric 1: local vicinity

<u>M2</u> (1069) Two joining sherds giving the full rim-section and the spout. 255g Diameter 330m 20%

Fabric: cream.

Inclusions: fairly frequent, ill-sorted, black, red-brown and quartz.

Trituration grit: black, red-brown and quartz.

Condition: made rough and powdery by weathering, with patches of discolouration.

<u>M4</u> (1219) Two joining sherds with complete spout. 520g Diameter 340mm 15%

Fabric: quite hard, fine-textured, drab cream fabric fired to pink near the surface under the flange and at the top of the outside surface; self-coloured.

Inclusions: fairly frequent, ill-sorted, mostly tiny and many small with few larger; mixed, quartz, red-brown and rare black material.

Trituration grit: small to medium, scattered randomly up to the bottom of the bead: mixed, red-brown sandstone, black rock and some quartz sandstone.

Condition: never used.

<u>M5</u> (1219) Two joining sherds giving the full rim-section. 110g Diameter 300mm 9%

Fabric: fairly hard, fine-textured, pinkish-cream with patches of orange-brown (possibly slip) on top of the flange, the inside of the bead and inside.

Inclusions: fairly frequent, minute to small with occasional larger grits, mostly red-brown, with some quartz and occasional black grits.

Trituration grit: ill-sorted, with distribution starting below the bead; red-brown sandstone, quartz and some black another material.

Condition: wear unknown because broken just below bead. Some faint cracking on upper surface of flange.

<u>M6</u> (1219) One small rim-fragment, giving full rim-section. 25g 3%

Fabric: fine-textured, cream with pale grey core; self-coloured, but may have some brownish slip on top of the flange.

Inclusions: fairly frequent, minute to small, with occasional larger particle; red-brown, quartz and fewer black.

<u>M11</u> (1622) Fragment with full rim-section. 70g Diameter 330mm 8%

Fabric: hard, slightly greyish-cream with pink in core.

Inclusions: moderate to fairly frequent, minute to small with few larger inclusions.

Trituration grit: included black and quartz.

Condition: greyish

Fabric 2: local vicinity, a variant of Fabric 1, possibly with different trituration grit.

<u>M12</u> (1208)   Three joining sherds giving full rim-section of a six-reeded, hammerhead rim, identical in form to Wilson 2002, fig 188, M106 which was made in the Mancetter-Hartshill potteries and which is dated in the report to AD240-350. This rim-profile is not only typical for the Mancetter-Hartshill potteries, but has never been recorded before in any other fabric. This Nostell example has one unusual feature; the surviving bodysherd shows what may be corrugation on the upper part of the body. Without more surviving we cannot know whether the whole exterior was corrugated or whether it was restricted to the upper part. Complete corrugation of the exterior was a technique rarely used in the Mancetter-Hartshill potteries and it would be unusual even to find it on the upper part. This term does not refer to the normal turning rings which occur on all mortaria, but to deliberate corrugation akin to the type often used on Rhineland mortaria (ibid. fig. 189, M115 and M117; the lines drawn in on fig.188, M90 are an example of an illustrator mistakenly drawing in ordinary turning rings.) 75g Diameter 330mm 8%

Fabric: Soft fine-textured, cream; self-coloured with a trace of what may have been a red-brown motif, perhaps a vertical or diagonal stripe of the type sometimes used as decoration on hammerhead type rims in the Mancetter-Hartshill potteries.

Inclusions: very moderate, ill-sorted, red-brown and black material with some quartz.

Trituration grit: only about three grits survive, all red-brown.

Condition: abraded, partly due to softness of fabric; some burning in a diagonal stripe across the rim near its fracture.

<u>M13</u> (1098) Three sherds (breaks could be modern) from a six-reeded, hammerhead mortarium of closely similar type to M12 but a different vessel. 75g Diameter 330mm 8.5%

Fabric: cream, possibly with self-coloured slip. Similar to the fabric of M12 but the texture is of a normal hardness.

Inclusions: similar to M12, but at least one streak of white clay and some white pellets (probably clay).

Trituration grit: none survives because of damage to the surface.

Condition: slight abrasion except on the inside where the surface has been completely abraded in some way.

Fabric 3: Mancetter-Hartshill potteries (Tomber and Dore 1998, 188-189)

<u>M15</u> (1031) One rim sherd from a five-reeded rim which is almost a wall-sided rim; the reeds are sharply and deeply incised; the upper wall surviving on M15 shows some corrugation at this point (corrugated exteriors are a highly exceptional feature in Mancetter-Hartshill mortaria – see above). These potteries did make wall-sided and near wall-sided forms but they never became popular like the hammerhead ones. This example would fit best amongst those made in the late second and earlier decades of the second century, cAD190-220 is probably the optimum date. The inside surface has been sheered off.

JOINS M16 in Context 1035 to create one rimsherd. 80g Diameter 340mm 5%

Fabric: hard, creamy white, with a self-coloured slip;

Inclusions: moderate, ill-sorted quartz with occasional orange-brown material;

Trituration grit: none survives on either M15 or M16.

<u>M16</u> (1035) One rimsherd joining M15.

Fabric 4: South Yorkshire, Cantley

<u>M18</u> (1094) Two joining rimsherds, joining two bodysherds from a mortarium with plain, narrow, diagonal rim of the type made at Cantley (Crageen 1957, fig 1, no.30 and Branton (Buckland 1976, fig.4, no.5); also see Doncaster (Buckland and Magilton 1986, fig 40, no.271). While the extent of the production period for this form is uncertain, it may be assumed to have been a long one. Related forms were being made by a Cantley potter who stamped VBRN?, sometimes interpreted as Virrinius? (see Crageen

1957, 367 and Wilson in prep (Newton Kyme) for discussion about this potter). Although these forms began to be made in the late second-century the main production was probably third century and it could have continued into the fourth. The red-brown decoration indicates a date later than 200; the terminal date of the production is uncertain. 115g. Diameter 240mm. 18% (1 extra body sherd, not necessarily a mortarium, but similar fabric: 5g)

Fabric: slightly granular, pale orange-brown fabric with cream slip and traces of red-brown decoration on the rim;

Inclusions: packed with rounded, transparent quartz, with very rare random darker grits;

Trituration grit: black, iron slag.

Condition: worn; surfaces slightly abraded.

Fabric 5: South Yorkshire, probably Cantley (Tomber and Dore 1998, 194)

M19 (1117) A rim sherd from a wall-sided mortarium with a bodysherd that belongs to the same vessel, but does not join. The rim-profile is similar to wall-sided forms produced at the Crambeck potteries cAD370-400 (Phillips and Heywood 1995, fig.126, no. 46), but wall-sided forms were being produced in the Oxford potteries from cAD240 (Young 1977, Fig 67, type C97). A date later than AD250 is likely for the Nostell example and late third or fourth-century is possible. 55g.Diameter 260. 6.5%

Fabric: orange-brown with mid grey core and traces of cream slip;

Inclusions: fairly frequent, but somewhat random, minute to tiny, quartz with rare black material; very rare quartz and dark larger inclusions;

Trituration grit: black iron slag with very very rare quartz

Condition: softish; wear uncertain.

3.3 A note on the samian pottery

Gwladys Monteil

Introduction

Most of the glossy red pottery known as samian was made in factories in France and Germany. The pottery is often highly decorative and the motifs used were frequently individual to a particular pottery, and some vessels can be traced to individual potters. Some of the main potteries (like at La Graufesenque and Lezoux in France and Rheinzabern in Germany) would export samian ware in massive quantities across the Roman Empire. Many pieces were brought to Britain and would be seen and used on dining tables across the (Romanised) land. Not only is samian useful for the purposes of dating assemblages but it is also an important indicator of the spread of Roman-style dining habits.

A total of 36 sherds of samian ware were recovered from excavations. The fabric of each sherd was examined, after taking a small fresh break, under a x20 binocular microscope and was catalogued by context number. Each archive entry consists of a context number, fabric, form and decoration identification, condition, sherd count, rim EVEs (Estimated Vessel Equivalents), rim diameter, weight, notes and a date range. The presence of wear, repair and graffiti was also systematically recorded. Rubbings of the decorated fragments were undertaken during analysis, which were mounted and scanned.

Samian pottery is highly standardised and specific pottery forms (i.e. different shapes of bowls, plates etc) are usually referred to by a generally established unique reference (e.g. 'Dr.31', which means a specific shape of undecorated dish or shallow bowl). Table 7 lists the forms present in this assemblage along with a brief explanation of the reference where relevant. The author would like to thank J. Bird for her help in identifying some of the decorated pieces.

The assemblage is small with 36 sherds for a total weight of 307g and a total rim EVES figure of 0.43 (Table 8). Most of the fragments are in poor condition with much of the original surfaces and slip poorly preserved. One dish has a repair lead rivet in situ, a Dr.31 in context [1261].

The assemblage

Despite its small size, the samian assemblage contains a range of fabrics and forms dating from the first to second century AD. Second century material dominates with Central Gaulish samian (Lezoux and Les Martres-de-Veyre) adding up to 30 sherds (Table 8). The range of forms is very limited with dishes and bowls dominating (Table 7). Unusually, cups are completely absent from this assemblage. The sherd count for the decorated form Dr.37 is relatively high but most of these sherds belong to the same bowl and there are in effect only three decorated vessels on the site.

Chronology

There is a little first century AD material but it is much abraded and lacking in diagnostic forms. One of the vessels could be pre to early Flavian (i.e. pre-69 AD or shortly thereafter) but the rest of the group is most probably Flavian (69-96 AD).

Determining an exact date range for the second century samian group is a little difficult considering the small size of the group. A very abraded and far from diagnostic sherd comes from the Trajanic (98-117 AD) industry of Les Martres-de-Veyre (context (1158), fill of well [1160]). The Central Gaulish decorated ware is Hadrianic and Antonine (117-138 and 138-192 AD). There is little later second century material, a few Dr.38 in pit [1401], a single un-diagnostic East Gaulish Dr.31 but there are no gritted mortaria, normally dated to post-170 AD, no examples of the form Dr.31R which dates from c.160 AD and no Walters 79 or 80. There is therefore nothing that is necessarily later than 170 AD.

South Gaulish

As mentioned above, first century AD samian material is scarce in this group and the South Gaulish group chiefly consists of plain forms. Much abraded, the fragments provide little information in terms of dating. Two relatively non-diagnostic forms could be identified: a dish form Dr.18 was recovered in gully [1202] that could be pre to early Flavian and a Dr.18/31 from the topsoil between Trenches 2 and 3 dating to the Flavian period.

Dish forms dominate the South Gaulish group which could fit with a military profile (Willis 2005, chart 13) though the absence of cups and decorated vessels prevent us from defining this assemblage

Form code	Description	No sherd	Weight (g)	rim EVE (Estimated Vessel Equivalents)
Dish	-	4	31	
Dragendorff 18 (DR18)	Plate, plain	1	8	0.06
DR18/31	Dish/shallow bowl, plain	1	8	0.05
DR31	Bowl, plain	4	36	0.145
DR18/31 or 31		1	8	
DR37	Bowl, decorated	14	172	0.175
DR38	Bowl, plain	5	28	
Unidentified	-	6	16	
Total	-	36	307	0.43

Table 7. Quantities of samian forms present

Fabric	No. of sherds	Weight (g)	Rim EVE (Estimated Vessel Equivalents)
South Gaulish	5	26	0.11
Martres-de-Veyre	1	1	
Central Gaulish	29	271	0.32
East Gaulish	1	9	
Total	36	307	0.43

Table 8. Quantities of samian fabrics present

as a typically military samian functional profile. The samian assemblage from phases I and II of the nearby Castleford fort includes a more diverse range of first century AD forms (Dickinson and Hartley 2000, 23 and Table 2) as does the group from Roecliffe fort (Dore 2005, 164).

Central Gaulish

The majority of the fragments are second century in date and come from Lezoux with 29 out of the 36 sherds (Table 8). The range is typical but limited with dishes of the Dr.18/31-31 family, at least five examples of the decorated bowl form Dr.37 and plain bowls Dr.38. As for the South Gaulish group, cup forms are absent.

A large proportion of the Central Gaulish material comes from the same feature (pit [1401]) which yielded 19 out of the 29 sherds. The plain samian group from pit [1401] consists of typically Antonine forms with dishes Dr.31 and flanged bowls Dr.38.

Nine sherds from the same decorated bowl form Dr.37 come from three consecutive fills of the pit (1400), (1413) and (1414). Though abraded, much of the decoration remains with panels separated by a very fine beaded line. The style can be attributed to the late Hadrianic-early Antonine Central Gaulish potter Birrantus ii (125-145 AD).

Three joining sherds from fill [1400] display an ovolo (small version of B108?), a fine beaded line (Rogers A1), a little leaf, a double circle and the motif Q6. There is a bowl from Regis House in London in the style of Birrantus ii (Mol 9689G) that displays a similar ovolo, the very fine beaded line, the leaf and the double circle. Motif Q6 is known for Birrantus ii (Rogers 1999, fig.12, no.2). The fragments from context [1414] also display motif Q6, the leaf and the fine beaded line but present more of the decoration with a very fragmentary festoon with an animal below. The festoon could be F42 registered for Birrantus ii (Rogers 1999) but there isn't enough left here to be certain. The animal seems to display a mane similar to one on a lion but none of the types listed by Oswald fits with this example. A tenth sherd from context [1772] could potentially be part of the same bowl; much abraded it seems to display a similar leaf motif.

The other stratified decorated fragment comes from context [1261]; its surface is very abraded which renders the identification difficult. The ovolo is particularly worn and the rest of the decoration consists of two types of leaf, the larger one could be H51, the small one J86 (?) both used by Cinnamus (145-180 AD).

The final fragment of decorated Central Gaulish ware from the site is unstratified. Little of the decoration remains, the two diamond-shaped motifs could be G66 (Rogers 1974) that were used by several Antonine potters.

Concluding remarks

In the light of the rest of the Roman pottery from the site (Leary, this volume), the very low quantities of first century AD samian is surprising and difficult to explain. Perhaps further excavation in the area will shed more light on this oddity.

In phases 3-5 the Romano-British pottery report clearly identifies the site of Nostell Priory as a rural settlement (Leary, this volume) and the low quantities of second century samian ware fit with the conclusion. The relative quantities of samian ware are nonetheless slightly higher than at other low-level rural sites in the area (Evans 2004, 18 and 32-3; Leary 2008, 29; Evans 2001b, 156, 158, 160, 170) and make this group fit with the upper end of the rural range in Yorkshire such as the site of Parlington Hollins (Evans 2001b, 160 and Table 8).

The lack of the two most popular cup forms, Dr.27 and Dr.33 in a group mostly dating to the second century AD when these two forms are the most popular type of cups is intriguing. A comparison with other samian groups from rural sites in West and South Yorkshire would suggest that the absence of cups is unusual though not unique (Evans 2001b, 156, 158, 160, 170; Ward 2008, Monteil 2010). In view of the small size of this group it is difficult to assess its significance and only a more comprehensive survey of samian form types recovered from rural sites in West and South Yorkshire might enhance our understanding of samian functional profiles from the area. The relative frequency of samian forms from rural sites in Britain generally is dominated by dish forms but includes cups (Willis 2005, chart 17).

3.4 Charred plant remains and charred wood remains

Ellen Simmons

Introduction

The excavations carried out in the new visitor car park revealed archaeological features primarily dating to the Romano-British period. Six soil samples, each of which was 10 litres in volume, were processed using a water separation machine for the recovery of charred plant remains and wood charcoal. Floating material was collected in sieves of 1mm and 300µm mesh, and the remaining heavy residue retained in a 1mm mesh. Processing and assessment of the samples was carried out by Angela Walker for On-Site Archaeology Ltd. As a result of this assessment it was decided that identification and analysis was to be carried out on wood charcoal and charred plant remains present in at the base of a corn-drier (1262) and a deposit at the base of a possible oven (1651).

The main aims of this analysis were to provide information concerning the agricultural economy of the site, the functions of the sampled features and the nature of the local environment. The following is an edited summary of the full report (Simmons 2012).

Summary of results

Cereal crops identified in a deposit at the base of the corn-drier (1262) included hulled barley, spelt wheat and free threshing wheat. Oat was also present but no chaff was recovered preventing the identification of the oat as either wild or cultivated. Seeds of cultivated flax were also recovered. Wild plant seeds associated with the cereal grains in the sample indicated the cultivation of heavy clay soils as well as autumn sowing of crops. A relatively high proportion of glume wheat chaff and grain sized weed seeds indicated the use of waste from the later stages of glume wheat crop processing as fuel. It is likely that the corn-drier was used for a number of purposes, including the drying of sheaves or ears of spelt wheat prior to storage or the parching of cereal grains prior to pounding and milling. Charcoal in the sample was dominated by

hazel, the ring curvatures of many of the fragments of which indicated the use of smaller branches, possibly from managed coppice woodland.

Tentative identification of heather stems in a sample from the base of a possible oven (1651) may indicate the burning of turfs as has been suggested at other Roman period sites in the region. The charcoal assemblage in the oven deposit was of a more mixed species composition and included Pomoideae (hawthorn group) possibly representing a less selective use of fuel wood in this context, change over time in the availably of fuel wood species or accumulation over a longer time period. The assemblage of charred plant remains included seeds of hawthorn and bramble as well as hazelnut shell, which may represent the collection of wild food resources. Cereals present included hulled barley and spelt wheat grains, which are likely to have been charred accidentally during food preparation or parching.

A full breakdown of the charred plant remains is given in Table 9 and the charcoal is summarised in Table 10.

Discussion

The suite of crops represented in samples from Nostell Priory is consistent with charred plant assemblages recovered from other Romano-British period sites in the region. Barley is the most commonly occurring cereal on Roman period sites in northern England with spelt wheat also being widely cultivated, especially towards the south of the region (Huntley 2002, 88). Bread wheat and emmer wheat have also been recovered at a number of sites and oats may also represent a significant crop, although this is difficult to determine due to problems in identifying cultivated from wild oat grains (Huntley 2002, 88).

The presence and proportions of charred plant material in the samples are however unlikely to be an exact representation of their original significance due to the skewing effects of the stage of crop processing at which the material was exposed to charring. The composition of crop remains in sample 9 (1262) from the base of the corn-drier is characteristic of a by-product from the later stages of glume wheat processing such as second winnowing, sieving with a medium coarse riddle or 'wheat sieve' and hand sorting (Hillman 1981: 132-137; Hillman 1984: 5). The sample was dominated by spelt wheat glume bases, spikelet forks and small or grain sized weed seeds, with a lower proportion of cereal grain. A review of charred plant remains recovered from Roman period corn-driers by van der Veen (1989) demonstrated that they may have been used for a variety of purposes, including drying of glume wheat sheaves or spikelets prior to storage or drying of grain prior to milling and malting of grains prior to brewing. Where large proportions of chaff are present this has been taken to indicate the use of crop processing waste as fuel that, where grains are also present, is mixed with material charred accidentally during crop drying.

Class	Species	Part	Sample 9 Context: (1262) Feature: Base of RB corn-drier	Sample 19 Context: (1651) Feature: Base of RB oven
Cereals and other economic plants	*Avena* indet (oat)	grains	6	
	cf. *Avena* indet	grains	6	3
	Hordeum sp. (barley)	hulled grains	6	1
		indet grains (straight)	2	
		indet grains	4	3
		chaff		
	cf. *Hordeum* sp.	indet grains	8	
	Free threshing *Triticum* sp.	grains	2	
	cf. free threshing *Triticum* sp.	grains	4	
	Free threshing *Triticum* sp. / *Triticum dicoccum* (free threshing wheat / emmer wheat)	grains	2	
	Free threshing *Triticum* sp. / *Triticum spelta* (free threshing wheat / spelt wheat)	grains	6	1
	Triticum spelta / dicoccum (spelt / emmer wheat)	grains		3
	Triticum spelta (spelt wheat)	grains	4	3
		glume bases	42	
	cf. *Triticum spelta*	grains	2	1
		glume bases	6	
	Free threshing *Triticum* sp. / *dicoccum* / *spelta* (free threshing wheat / emmer wheat / spelt wheat)	grains	8	2
	Triticum sp. (wheat)	grains	6	2
		glume bases	36	3
	Cereal indet	grains	4	
		> 2mm culm node	2	
		Cereal grain and > 2mm Poaceae (grass family) grain fragments (non embryo ends)	42	5
		Bud scale indet.		7
		Parenchyma (undifferentiated plant storage tissue)	2	

Table 9. Charred plant remains

		Vesicular indeterminate material	74	29
		Organic amalgam	4	
	Linum usitatissimum L. (flax)		2	
	Corylus avellana L. (hazel)	nut shell fragment		1
Wild / weed plant seeds	*Ranunculus* cf. *flammula* (lesser spearwort)		2	4
	Papaver rhoeas / dubium (common / long-headed poppy)	immature seed heads		36
	Urtica dioica L. (common nettle)		2	
	Chenopodium album L. (fat hen)		2	2
	Caryophyllaceae indet. (pink family)		2	
	Stellaria graminea L. (lesser stitchwort)		2	
	Spergula arvensis L. (corn spurrey)			2
	Silene latifolia Poir. (white campion)		2	
	Rumex acetosella L. (sheep's sorrel)			8
	Rumex crispus / obtusifolius (curled / broad-leaved dock)		10	
	Rumex conglomeratus / sanguineus (clustered / wood dock)		2	
	Rubus fruticosus agg. (bramble)			1
	Potentilla sp. (cinquefoil)		2	
	Crataegus monogyna Jacq. (hawthorn)			2
	Vicia / Lathyrus spp. (vetch / wild pea)		4	
	Medicago / Trifolium sp. (medick / clover)		2	
	Plantago media L. (hoary plantain)			1
	Veronica officinalis L. (heath speedwell)		2	
	Galium aparine L. (cleavers)		6	
	Anthemis cotula L. (stinking chamomile)		10	
	Carex spp. (ovoid)			4
	> 2mm Poaceae (large grass family)		8	4
	< 2mm Poaceae (small grass family)		34	18
	Bromus secalinus L. (Brome grass)		26	5
	cf. *Bromus secalinus*		22	2
	Indeterminate wild / weed seed		26	28

Table 9. Charred plant remains (continued)

Wood species present	Sample 9 Context: (1262) Feature: Base of RB corn-drier	Sample 19 Context: (1651) Feature: Base of RB oven
Ulmus sp. (elm)		1 (0.036g)
Quercus sp. (oak)	5 (0.162g)	19 (0.441g)
Alnus glutinosa L. (alder)	1 (0.026g)	2 (0.082g)
Corylus avellana L. (hazel)	36 (0.604g)	13 (0.481g)
Populus / Salix (poplar / willow)	1 (0.021g)	
Pomoideae (hawthorn group)		6 (0.164g)
Acer campestre L. (field maple)		1 (0.015g)
Fraxinus excelsior L. (ash)	6 (0.265g)	
Indeterminate	1 (0.023g)	8 (0.121g)
Total number / weight of fragments	50 (0.157g)	50 (1.340g)

Table 10. Charred wood
Total number and weight of charcoal fragments in grams (figure in brackets) in each sample by species

Ethnographic evidence suggests that, in wet climates, glume wheats would have been stored as spikelets following threshing, winnowing and coarse sieving (Hillman 1984, 153-154). This would have protected them from pests and diseases while in storage. Further processing, involving parching and pounding to release the grain from the spikelets, followed by further winnowing and sieving to remove the chaff and weed seeds would have been carried out on a piecemeal, possibly daily, basis when necessary. The by-products of these later stages of processing are particularly likely to come into contact with fire and as such would be expected to form a major component of the charred plant assemblage.

The predominance of chaff in sample 9 (1262) along with lower proportions of cereal grain and grain sized weed seeds is similar to the composition of charred plant assemblages at other Romano-British period settlement sites in the region. At the Iron Age/Romano-British site of Dalton Parlours near Tadcaster a large assemblage of charred plant remains was recovered from various contexts within Romano-British structures at the site. This assemblage was composed of high proportions of spelt wheat glume bases in comparison to spelt wheat grains and large numbers of weed seeds including brome grass. Much of the material was interpreted as the burning of crop processing waste as fuel. Bread wheat grains and rachis internodes, six row hulled barley grains and rachis internodes, oats and seed of cultivated flax was also present. (Murray 1990, 189-194).

At a Romano-British farmstead excavated at Thurnscoe, South Yorkshire, spelt wheat predominated along with small quantities of emmer wheat and free-threshing wheat while six row hulled barley and oats were also present. Large quantities of glume wheat chaff and grain sized weed seeds were interpreted as charred waste from the final stages of crop processing (Giorgi 2004, 64-70). A corn-drier also excavated at the site was interpreted as being used for the parching of glume wheats prior to pounding or the drying of grain prior to storage or milling as well as the roasting of germinated grain (Giorgi 2004, 71). At Parlington Hollins East, excavated as part of the M1-A1 Link Road Scheme, spelt wheat, barley and emmer wheat were present, with a high proportion of chaff (Young and Richardson 2001, 221-223).

The charred assemblage in sample 19 (1651) recovered from the base of a possible oven was composed largely of grain with very little chaff. This may be due in part to poor preservation, cereal grains surviving charring more readily than chaff (Boardman and Jones 1990). The charred grains are likely to represent material that was accidentally burnt during food preparation or parching. The immature seed heads of common / long headed poppy present in this sample may represent weed seed heads which are generally removed from the crop during the earlier stages of processing and used as fuel (Hillman 1984, 5). The tentative identification of heather stems in this sample may represent the use of heather or turfs as a fuel (Hall and Huntley 2007, 213). Heather was identified in a sample from the Romano-British settlement site at Thurnscoe and interpreted as being used for tinder (Gale 2004, 79). The presence of hawthorn seeds may be related to the use of *Pomoideae* wood as fuel or may represent berries collected as food. A seed of bramble and a fragment of hazelnut shell may represent the collection of wild food resources.

The majority of wild plant species represented were associated with arable or disturbed ground and due to their association with cereal grains, are likely to have derived from weeds that were harvested along with the crops. The presence of stinking mayweed has been taken as an indicator of the cultivation of heavier clay soils and is frequently recovered at Romano-British sites in Yorkshire (Huntley 2002, 90). The presence of cleavers suggests autumn sowing of cereals as it is an autumn germinating weed. Other sources of charred wild plant seeds include waste roofing or flooring material, kindling and turfs burnt as fuel. It is possible that the seeds of grassland and heath taxa present in both samples may have originated in turfs burnt as fuel.

The assemblage of wood charcoal in the two samples is also likely to be biased by taphonomic factors such as the preferential selection of certain species for a variety of purposes as well as factors such as differential preservation (Théry-Parisot, Chabal & Chrzavzez 2010). The range of woody plant species represented therefore is unlikely to be an accurate reflection of those present in the environment. The presence of woodland tree species such as ash, elm and oak does suggest that some open woodland may be present nearby. Pollen records for the area are somewhat sparse but do generally indicate major woodland clearance beginning in the Iron Age and continuing into the Roman period (Dark 1999, 259). Pollen recovered from a buried soil beneath a Roman road at Roman Ridge on the M1-A1 link was affected by pollen assemblage mixing but indicated a predominantly open landscape prior to the construction of the road (Long and Tipping 2001, 225). Charcoal recovered from Thurnscoe included oak and maple along with hazel, birch, alder and blackthorn. The combination of oak, birch and heather was interpreted as a possible indicator of local open woodland (Gale 2004, 79). The presence of alder indicates damp soils or a watercourse in the vicinity of the site.

The oak, ash and elm charcoal in these samples may therefore represent coppiced standards in managed woodland, hedgerows or scrub. It is likely that much of the local woodland that was still present by the Roman period was managed. This interpretation

would be supported by the ring curvatures of the charcoal fragments, the majority of which indicate the use of smaller branches (Marguerie & Hunot 2007, 1421) although no direct evidence for coppicing was noted during the charcoal identification. Wood recovered from Roman Castleford appeared to suggest local woodland management due to its uniform nature (Bastow 1999, 176). The dimensions of hazel round wood recovered from Thurnscoe suggested the use of coppice (Gale 2004, 78).

Oak, ash and elm are all excellent structural timbers. Where pollarded or coppiced these species, alongside hazel and willow, produce poles that can be used for wattle fencing. Maple is good for carving utilitarian objects. Offcuts from the use of timber for structural or utilitarian purposes would have been utilised as fuel or wood may have been gathered or cut specifically for burning.

The differences in composition of the charcoal assemblage between the two samples from Nostell Priory may be related to the function of the contexts. The use of primarily hazel, likely from managed coppice, in the corn-drier context, sample 9 (1262) may be related to the suitability of hazel as a fuel wood. The more mixed assemblage from the possible oven context sample 19 (1651) may indicate a less selective use of fuels which included a relatively significant proportion of hedgerow, woodland edge or scrub type woody species. The presence of small round wood twigs in this sample, tentatively identified as heather or ling (cf. Ericaceae) may also indicate the use of turfs as fuel. The greater species diversity of material from the 'oven' deposit may also however be related to changes in the availability of certain woody fuel species over time as well as possibly being the result of a longer period of accumulation than the material recovered from the corn-drier (Théry-Parisot, Chabal & Chrzavzez 2010, 144).

3.5 Ceramic building material and daub

Sophie Tibbles

Introduction

As well as daub (unfired clay used in conjunction with wooden wattling to create walls or other structures), the excavation produced a number of fragments of brick or tile of Romano-British date. The presence of such material is highly significant as it indicates the presence of higher status buildings or structures. This is an edited version of the full report (Tibbles 2011).

The assemblage

Romano-British ceramic building material (CBM) forms were recorded within eight contexts (Table 11), in the form of roof tiles (*tegulae*), bricks, a fragment of box-flue and a further 15 non-identifiable fragments that may have been brick or tile. The assemblage of daub/fired clay was recovered from fourteen Romano-British contexts (Table 12).

Roof Tile – Tegulae

Fourteen fragments of *tegulae* were recorded (weight 2118 grams), some of which displayed remnants of the finger-smoothed original edges of the top or bottom of the tile or patches of knife-smoothing. The thickness of the tiles ranged between 21mm and 29mm. Two fragments displayed means of suspension in the form of a finger-smoothed flange, Type 11 (1283) and an upper cut-away (1023). Three joining fragments were recorded from the secondary fill (1776) of ditch [1778]. A total of eight individual tiles were tentatively identified.

Brick

The brick assemblage consisted of fifteen fragments with a weight of 4356 grams. All were recovered from ditch fill (1776). Based on thickness, which ranged between 28mm and 31mm, thirteen fragments were categorised as *bessales* (square Roman bricks of 198mm). Finger-smoothed original edges were recorded on nine fragments, of which five could be identified as corners. The remaining two (conjoining) fragments were identified as a *pedalis* (a larger square brick of 281mm square). The pedalis had a thickness of 37mm and a weight of 205 grams. Knife-smoothing was noted on the upper surface and breaks were crisp and fresh.

Box-Flue Tile

One fragment of box-flue tile was identified from the fill (1163) of pit [1164]. The characteristic feature of combing for the adhesion of plaster was evident; a single vertical stroke of five tines. The tile was broken at the returning edge, though some remnants of the plain face were noted.

Daub

Seventy-five fragments of daub/fired clay were identified in Romano-British contexts with nearly 30% of the assemblage in primary fill [1219] of

Context	Context Interpretation	Phase/ date of context	No. of Fragments
1023	Fill of ditch [1010/1018/1024/1055/1057]	Phase 2: late 1st –early 2nd century	1
1037	Subsoil	Unstratified	2
1069	Secondary fill of ditch [1071/1085/1100/1195]	Phase 5: late 3rd -mid 4th century	2
1163	Fill of oval pit [1164]	Undated	1
1219	Primary fill of linear ditch [1251]	Phase 2: late 1st –early 2nd century	1
1283	Fill of linear ditch 1104/[1284]	Phase 5: late 3rd -mid 4th century?	4
1773	Bank	Medieval	1
1776	Secondary fill of broad shallow linear ditch [1778]	Medieval	33
TOTAL			45

Table 11. Ceramic building material (CBM) by context

Context	Context interpretation	Phase of feature	Number of fragments
1069/1098	Secondary fill of ditch [1071/1085/1100/1195]	Phase 5: late 3rd -mid 4th century	19
1117	Secondary fill of linear ditch [1119]	Phase 5: late 3rd -mid 4th century	1
1158	Secondary fill of pit/well [1160]	Phase 2: late 1st –early 2nd century	10
1167	Backfill of clay lined pit [1168]	Phase 3: Mid to late 2nd century	2
1169	Fill of oval pit [1170]	Undated	4
1219	Primary fill of linear ditch [1251]	Phase 2: late 1st –early 2nd century	23
1523	Primary fill of circular posthole [1524]	Undated	1
1563	Final fill of sub-oval pit [1566]	Undated	1
1638	Subsoil	Unstratified	6
1644	Fill of oven/corn-drier [1639]	Phase 2: late 1st –early 2nd century	1
1646	Upper fill of oven/corn-drier [1639]	Phase 2: late 1st –early 2nd century	2
1668	Fill of rectangular posthole [1669]	Undated	1
1760	Fill of oval posthole [1761]	Phase 2: late 1st –early 2nd century	4
Total			75

Table 12. Daub by context

ditch [1251]. Discolouration from heat exposure was recorded on forty-five pieces. It is worthy of note that of these fragments, the surfaces of twenty-eight were 'over-fired' and almost vitrified in appearance. This would be indicative of high temperatures or prolonged exposure to direct heat.

Discussion

The majority of the Romano-British CBM was residual, recovered from (1776), the fill of a medieval ditch that was found during the excavation of the new footpath to the visitor car park (the investigation of the footpath area is not reported on in this volume because no Romano-British or Iron Age features were found there. Non-Romano-British/ Iron Age features are reported in OSA 2009). It lay just to the northwest of the church, over 200m from the main car park excavation. The material must have been re-deposited during the medieval period either when it was excavated from its original place of deposition – the clean breaks would indicate that the material would not have been moved far - or, possibly, because the Roman bricks had been re-used in a later, medieval, building. This was not an uncommon practice (Ryan 1996, 1), particularly within ecclesiastical buildings as, for example, at St

Botolph's Priory, Colchester, and St Albans Abbey (Wright 1972, 15).

The box-flue tile could indicate a building with a heating system was in the vicinity of the investigation. The *bessales* would also support this hypothesis, as they were mainly used to construct hypocaust pillars (*pilae*) (Brodribb 1987, 34). A hypocaust heating system would suggest a building of high status/affluence. Although there is a lack of evidence to support a military presence, such as legionary stamps, it could be tentatively suggested that the high status/affluent building *may* have been associated with a military settlement. De la Bédoyère suggests that bath houses were constructed "away from villa houses or forts" (1991, 33) such as at Malton (Wenham and Haywood 1997, 3) and at Dalton Parlours (Wrathmell and Nicholson 1990, 281).

The daub/fired clay could have served a number of uses. The assemblage may have originated from wattle and daub walls or partitions, or a smaller free-standing structures such as a hearth or an oven. The original surfaces noted would suggest that the latter examples are more likely. The assemblage probably represents dumping of material associated with occupational activity. It could be tentatively suggested that some of the material may be associated with oven [1639], but this is impossible to prove and it should be noted that the three small fragments of daub recovered from the feature exhibited no signs of direct heat so it is unlikely that they were part of the feature's superstructure.

3.6 Other finds

The other finds summarised here (quernstones, glass and metalwork) have been fully reported on elsewhere (OSA 2009). The original reports are referenced in each section as appropriate.

Quernstones

Four querns or quern fragments were recovered during the excavation, consisting of one beehive quern in excellent condition (Q1), two fragments of upperstones from Romano-British flat disc-type rotary querns (Q2 and Q3) and one fragment of lower stone from a rotary quern (Q4) (Table 13). The beehive quern and the lower stone fragment were found during topsoil stripping and were unstratified. The two upper stone fragments from rotary querns were from Romano-British contexts. Most interestingly one of the two rotary querns is an unusual local type with twin opposed hoppers and early military associations. This is an edited version of the full report (Pinnock 2011) incorporating comments from John Cruse, Yorkshire Archaeological Society Quern Coordinator, particularly regarding twin-hopper type military querns).

Description

Quern 1 is an upper stone of a beehive quern with a flat grinding surface, twin opposed handle sockets, a feed pipe and a hopper (Plate 17 and Figure 24, Q1). The two horizontal cylindrical handle sockets are on opposite sides of the quern. Neither handle socket pierces the feed pipe making this a 'Yorkshire' rather than a 'Hunsbury' type (Philips 1950). The hopper is V-shaped in profile with a pronounced collar. The circular feed pipe has a slight lip 40mm up from bottom where it was drilled in opposite directions. The grinding face is still fresh and coarse apart from a worn band around the edge up to 25mm wide. The quern was fractured in antiquity at the site of one of the handle sockets, removing a part of the grinding face. This quern was found during topsoil stripping on the northern edge of the access road, close to but not associated with feature [1279], and is consequently unstratified.

Quern 2 is a fragment of a relatively thin upper stone from a rotary quern. It is about a fifth of a complete

Quern number	Context	Type	Condition	Phase/ date of context	Note
Q1	U/S	Beehive upper stone of millstone grit	Excellent near complete	N/A	Found in topsoil- Deliberately destroyed in antiquity
Q2	(1083) fill of ditch [1071/1085/1100/1195]	Fragment of upper stone of rotary quern of millstone grit	Approx. 20% fragment	Phase 5: late 3rd -mid 4th century	Not particularly diagnostic fragment
Q3	(1167) fill of pit [1168]	Fragment of upper stone of twin-hopper rotary quern of millstone grit	Approx. 20% fragment	Phase 3: Mid to late 2nd century	Rare type with military associations
Q4	U/S	Rotary quern lower stone of millstone grit	Approx. 15% fragment	N/A	Not particularly diagnostic fragment-Probably Romano-British date

Table 13. Contents of the quernstone assemblage

Plate 17. Quern 1 as found on site

stone. The hopper is crudely shaped and is roughly dished. There is moderate wear visible over the entire grinding surface. This was found in the backfill of boundary ditch [1071/1085/1100/1195] along with pottery from the late third to fourth century AD.

Quern 3 is a fragment of a rare type of rotary hand quern that has two opposed D-shaped hoppers (Figure 24, Q3). The grinding surface would have been an estimated 380mm in diameter and the stone is 72 mm thick at the edge. The fragment shows a very steeply inclined hopper (37mm deep) that is well shaped and a flat topped rim 35mm wide. There is slight wear visible over the entire grinding surface.

The two opposed D-shaped hoppers would have been separated by a flat 'bar' into which was set a central perforation to receive the spindle. Within each hopper typically was a D-shaped feedpipe. These querns are usually a little larger than is estimated here, and a diameter of something like 400-420mm might be more typical. Seven relatively intact examples are known from the Yorkshire Quern Survey, along with a further fourteen fragments. Where dated, they are typically second to third century, are predominately of millstone grit and have a distribution focused on the eastern side of the Pennine 'military zone' (Doncaster, Castleford & Newton Kyme), often being found on sites with military connections. A working hypothesis is that they are a regionally specific type, manufactured locally by contractor(s) for use by auxiliaries, but with a proportion leaking out into associated civil sites (John Cruse *pers comm*). This example was found in the backfill of a rectangular clay-lined pit/cistern [1168] along with a large assemblage of pottery dated to the mid to late second century AD.

Quern 4 is a fragment of lower stone, likely to belong to a rotary quern rather than a beehive type due to its flat, well-crafted, shape. Its size suggests that it may match either Quern 2 or 3, although as it was unstratified this cannot be confirmed. This quern was found during topsoil stripping with a mechanical excavator in the western part of the main car park.

Discussion

Beehive querns were becoming common by the fourth century BC and possibly in the fifth century (Heslop 2008). In some cases beehive querns continued to be used into the Roman period (Chadwick

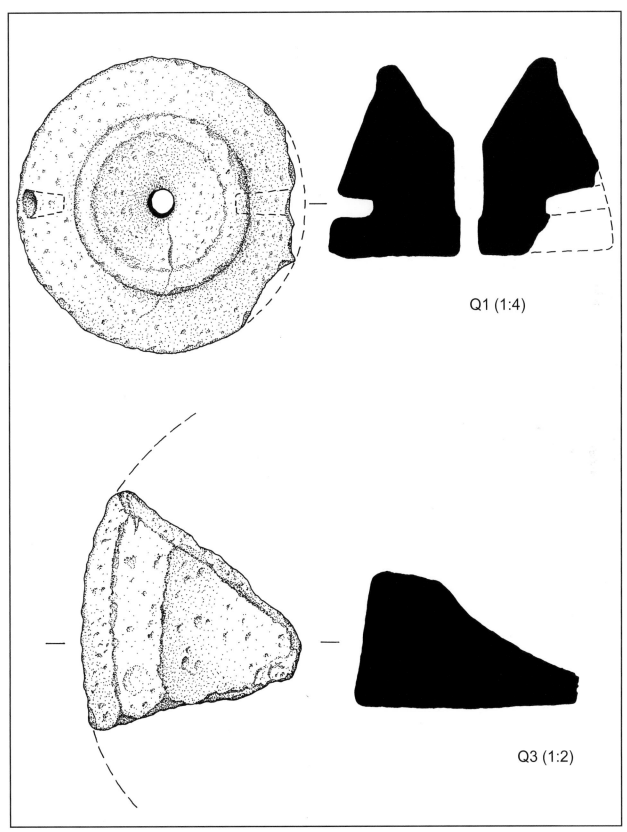

Q1 (1:4)

Q3 (1:2)

Figure 24. Querns 1 and 3

2009, Wright 1996). Although they were largely replaced by rotary querns in the south of England, stratified examples from Dalton Parlours demonstrate that beehive querns were in use alongside flat disc types into the third and fourth centuries AD in this region (Buckley and Major 1990). Beehive querns have also found alongside flat disc querns at the otherwise Romano-British dated site of Apple Tree Close, Pontefract (Turner 1987) and at Castleford (Buckley and Major 1998). The damage to the beehive quern (Q1) is likely to have been a deliberate act to put the quern out of use, a frequent occurence with beehive querns (Heslop 2008). Together with the presence of at least one corn-drier of Romano-British date and two undated 'four-post structures' (often interpreted as Iron Age-style grain stores) the querns provide further evidence for the on site processing of cereals, potentially from the pre-Roman Iron Age (possibly Quern 1), through the mid-late second century (Quern 3), potentially until the late third to early fourth century (Quern 2).

Quern 3 is an unusual type and assumes greater importance in the context of this site due to its Roman military associations. Along with the evidence of the pottery on the site, the quern reinforces the 'military' aspect of the site. Found in backfill dating to the mid to late second century, the quern was deposited in phase 3 of the site and this date fits with the other occurrences of the type in the region. However, phase 3 is not otherwise associated with the military and it is only in phase 2 that a military connection is indicated by the pottery assemblage. It is, though, quite possible that the quern fragment was residual when incorporated in the backfill of the clay-lined pit/cistern (use of which, as opposed to its backfilling, is thought to date from the military phase) and that it may indeed date from the Flavian-Trajanic period, an interpretation that would better fit with the other military remains in that period on this site (though not the dating of the other known querns of this type).

Glass

The investigation produced a small assemblage of glass (Bruce 2011). The majority of pieces were recovered from features dated through pottery to the Roman period (Table 14). Most are small body fragments from vessels, probably bottles. SF 17 is a more interesting and is the largest single fragment in the assemblage, probably being from a handle of a bottle.

Glass number	Context	Type	Phase/ date of context	Note
SF 17	(1028) the fill of pit [1030]	Fragment of glass vessel	Phase 5: late 3rd -mid 4th century	Fragment of glass vessel. Part of a broad strap handle, maximum 48mm wide and 7mm thick. Some exterior decoration. The glass had a light green colour. Probably from a Roman bottle.
SF 18	(1070) fill of ditch [1071/1085/1100/1195]	Fragment of glass waste?	Phase 5: late 3rd -mid 4th century	Dark green colour. Maximum length 18mm.
SF 19	(1262) fill of corndrier [1265]	Two very small fragments of glass vessel?	Phase 3: Mid to late 2nd century	Body of a square or polygonal bottle or flask in pale green glass. Max 17mm long, 5mm thick
SF 20	(1227) fill of pit [1218]	Small fragment of glass?	Phase 5: late 3rd -mid 4th century	Opaque dark blue / purple. Maximum of 9mm across and 4mm thick. Possible vessel fragment or part of an inlay from a composite object.
SF 21	(1381) fill of ditch [1203/1383]	Fragment of vessel glass	Phase 2: late 1st –early 2nd century	Blue green colour. Maximum length 28mm, 5mm thick. Hint of an angle suggesting it is from a square or polygonal bottle or similar vessel

Table 14. Content of glass assemblage

Metal finds

Summary

Sixteen small finds (9 iron and 7 copper alloy) were recovered from the excavation and submitted for conservation analysis (Tables 15 and 16). All were x-rayed and examined under a binocular microscope at X20 magnification (Panter 2010, K.Kenward 2012). The material identifications were checked and observations made about the condition of the finds. Most of the objects were fragments of nail, which are relatively common finds, or other unidentifiable metal fragments. There were four objects of more potential interest, but they were very poorly preserved.

SF no	Context	Assessment
1	1388	Labelled as "Fe nail". Encrusted with soil and dense brown corrosion products. No signs of active corrosion, nail is stable, and in a fair condition. X-ray shows that a substantial metal core survives although pitted and complete mineralisation of the nail tip.
2	1117	Labelled as "Fe". Four fragments encrusted with soil, charcoal flecks and orange/brown corrosion products. No signs of active corrosion, objects are stable. X-ray shows 1 x nail shank, 1 x tack and 2x fragments, all completely mineralised but in a fair condition.
3	1005	Labelled as "Fe". Four nail fragments: one fragment is large corrosion blister that has become detached from nail head. All are covered with orange/brown corrosion products, no evidence for active corrosion and nails are stable. X-ray reveals all fragments to be completely mineralised, overall fair condition.
4	1001	Labelled as "Fe". Large nail shank, incomplete. Evidence of previous active corrosion on broken ends, but now stable. Encrusted with soil and dense orange and brown corrosion products. X-ray reveals a pitted but substantial metal core surviving, overall fair condition.
5	1407	Labelled as "Fe". Two nail shank fragments which join together. Encrusted with soil and orange/brown corrosion products and large corrosion blisters. Mineral preserved plant material visible, derived from the burial deposit. Broken ends show core is voided and X-ray reveals complete mineralisation. Stable and fair condition.
6	1123	Labelled as "Fe obj." Comprising 5 fragments which X-ray confirms as two nail shanks and 3 detached flakes. Poor condition with evidence for active corrosion. Several longitudinal cracks present and X-ray shows that a substantial metallic core survives although pitted.
7	1011	Labelled as "Fe obj.". X-ray confirms as large nail shank, encrusted with voluminous dense brown corrosion products. No signs of active corrosion, nail is stable. Several longitudinal cracks present, but X-ray shows a substantial metallic core remaining, although pitted. Fair condition.
8	1526	Labelled as "Iron Nail". 3 fragments which X-ray confirms as two shank fragments (which join) and one stone. Both fragments are completely mineralised with no core remaining. Poor condition, but stable.
9	1129	Labelled as "Fe Obj.". Knife blade, with tang missing. Large corrosion blister at tang end, and knife is encrusted with pale orange/brown corrosion products. No evidence for active corrosion, X-ray shows almost complete mineralisation, but blade is stable.

Table 15. Conservation assessment of iron objects

SF no	Context	Assessment
10	--	Labelled as "Lead? Cu". Fragment is encrusted with green copper and pale grey lead corrosion products. X-ray image is very dense and weight of fragment suggests a copper alloy with a high lead content. Probable casting waste piece. Fair condition.
11	1156	Labelled as "Cu alloy object". Possible sheet fragment with large perforation, plus two tiny fragments. Poor condition with traces of a black patinated surface disrupted by powdery pale green corrosion products. X-ray shows little metal survives.
13	1720	Labelled as "Coin?" In 3 fragments, very poor condition, numerous cracks present and encrusted with soil and green, black and cuprite corrosion products. X-ray suggests object is a coin but inscription is illegible, and completely mineralised. Due to poor condition further investigation is unlikely to clarify any surviving traces of the inscription. Hence no further work.
14	1261	Labelled as "Cu obj.". Probable fitting with inlaid crescent of blue glass. Possible enamel obscured by soil. Patinated but broken edges reveal powdery green corrosion products; object is actively corroding and unstable. X-ray shows some metal remaining.
16	1400	Labelled as "Copper fragments". 5 x possible sheet fragments and 1 rivet. Poor condition completely mineralised with powdery green corrosion products on broken edges. Unstable.
--	1457	Labelled as "Cu coin". X-ray confirms as possible coin but inscription is illegible. Poor condition, cracked but metallic core survives, although heavily mineralised. Encrusted with green and black copper corrosion products and an area of bare metal is visible.
--	1263	Labelled as "Cu brooch". Poor condition, having remains of a patinated surface in places but elsewhere the surface has been lost to expose dark green corrosion products. Catch plate is missing. X-ray shows substantial metallic core surviving.

Table 16. Conservation assessment of copper alloy objects

Discussion

Of the two possible coins, coin SF13 from (1720), the fill of a pit from the early Romano-British phase 2 was too broken and corroded to merit further investigation. However a coin from context (1457), the fill of posthole [1458], one of a number of postholes just to the east of the well and clay-lined pits, was examined further. After cleaning, a photograph of the coin was sent to Craig Barclay who notes: "It is a counterfeit denarius. It dates from the late C2nd to early C3rd AD. Not 100% certain, but probably based on a coin of Septimius Severus." (Plate 18.)

The brooch from context (1263) – the lining of corn-drier [1265], dated to phase 3, the mid to late second century - was severely corroded leading to break up of the patinated surface (Plate 19). The form of the brooch was obscured by a layer of soil lying over patches of dark patina. The soil crust and patina were missing from large areas revealing dark green corrosion products with bright, powdery active corrosion below. The catch plate had broken off and was missing. During cleaning patches of a bright white metal coating (silver or tin plating or a surface enhancement) was observed.

A similar pattern of corrosion had occurred to fitting SF14 from (1261), the backfill of the same corn-drier which has been dated to the subsequent phase 4/third century (Plate 20). The fitting is 11mm long and there is a crescent of blue glass visible, which appears in good condition with possibly more enamel concealed by the overlying soil. There are fragments of two loops through the hoop on the reverse, which are broken at both ends revealing active blue/green corrosion. On removing the soil, cells of very weathered, fragile, yellow glass were revealed either side of the blue crescent. A dark substance is also present in the end grooves, more in the right hand one then the left. This also appears to be very decayed glass.

Knife SF9 from (1129), the fill of otherwise undated posthole [1130], was found to have a hint of poorly defined mineral preserved organics (remains of a wooden handle?) on one side at the tang end.

Plate 18. Counterfeit denarius (photo: York Archaeological Trust)

Plate 19. Roman brooch (photo: York Archaeological Trust)

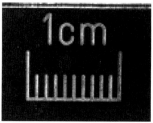

Plate 20. Fitting with crescent of blue glass (photo: York Archaeological Trust)

Part 4
Discussion and Concluding Remarks

4.1 Discussion

The nature of the occupation

Phase 1. Pre-Roman Iron Age: a possible native settlement

With the exception of one feature, there is a degree of doubt regarding the existence of occupation in the pre-Roman Iron Age (PRIA) at Nostell. Although a number of features have been tentatively dated to the Iron Age, and this early period has been described as a separate phase analytically, period assignment has been made on the basis of pottery dating alone. The sole exception is the very large north-south orientated ditch [1220] glimpsed only in the access road, which is also dated on stratigraphic grounds. The problem with dating by pottery alone is that handmade vessels of Iron Age types continued in use on rural sites until the early second century, so pottery alone is of limited use in distinguishing a pre-Romano-British phase. The argument could be made that the apparently exclusively military nature of the pottery assemblage (albeit with less samian pottery than might be expected) from the first Romano-British phase (dating to the late first and early second century) on this particular site would have precluded the continued use of handmade wares. It would be unusual indeed to find the Roman military using 'native' Iron Age-style pottery alongside Roman pottery. However, as Leary (this volume) points out it is quite possible that the pots might have been acquired for their contents and quickly discarded once emptied. There is an appropriately small number of sherds (a total of just 23) to make this a realistic scenario. There are no other finds to help further, and even the unstratified beehive quernstone cannot be said to be definitely Iron Age in date. In the south of England such a quern might be taken as evidence of Iron Age occupation but beehive querns continue to be used in the north into the third and fourth centuries AD (e.g. Buckley and Major 1990).

If the possible Iron Age features are genuinely pre-Roman, they record the presence of a small-scale field system with irregular, triangular fields or paddocks enclosed by small ditches, a hedge and possibly by a line of postholes and small pits (possibly also postholes) generally trending from southeast to northwest. In the Iron Age phase at Dalton Parlours near Tadcaster, small gullies of a similar scale were sometimes found subdividing larger enclosures defined by large ditches (e.g. in Enclosure VII, Wrathmell and Nicholson 1990). The attribution of ditch [1331] to this phase is questionable, but if so it would be of a similar scale to some of the large field boundary/enclosure ditches at Dalton Parlours. This is also true of the very large ditch [1220], which is the best dated Iron Age (or earlier) feature on account of its deep, gradually accumulated, fills being recut by a well-dated early Romano-British ditch. This feature may have been in existence for hundreds of years before being re-cut in the early Roman phase, at a point when it was a much reduced surface feature, mostly infilled by gradual erosion – presumably of an associated bank. The site at Nostell Priory may have formed part of the agricultural zone of a settlement in the near vicinity, possibly similar in nature to the fields and enclosures found at South Elmsall some 6 miles to the southeast (Esmonde Cleary 1998). The primary divisions of the landscape trend northeast-southwest and northwest-southeast but are mainly irregular. This may either imply a disregard for regularity in the minds of the people who created this landscape, or that the landscape was occasionally re-organised during the course of this phase giving the impression of irregularity as a result of the 'overwriting' of earlier features by later ones.

The only clue to the location of any settlement might be the substantial post setting in the access road (posthole [1282]) and the three nearby but undated pits [1246], [1248], and [1643], which may speculatively point to a settlement area to the north. The undated four-post structures found in the northern part of the main car park are also probably of Iron

Age date (see below) and may have been placed on the edge of any settlement as was the case at Castle Hills site M near Garforth (Brown et al. 2007).

Phase 2. The early Romano-British period: an undiscovered fort?

The earliest Romano-British phase dating to the late first to early second centuries is of regional significance (with national implications) due to the unusual character of the ceramic assemblage indicating that the site was military related. A number of aspects of the ceramic assemblage point towards this conclusion.

The first is the nature of the wares and the types of vessels found on site. A range of Flavian-Trajanic (69-117 AD) forms were present (an amphora, flagons, beakers, "honey-pots", rusticated jars, reeded-rim bowls, white ware bowls and painted beakers) - a combination strongly suggestive of pottery production for use by the Roman military. At this early date local native settlements were simply unable (and/or unwilling) to access large quantities or a wide range of Roman vessels, continuing to rely on handmade pottery of Iron Age type supplemented by occasional Roman pots. Although many of the vessels seem to have been produced locally (see below), two jars appear to have been produced at the military fort of Doncaster while the early samian was produced in Gaul, both strongly indicative of military supply lines, given the early date of the assemblage. Leary concludes from her analysis of the assemblage, "the quantity and range of vessels implies a military related site, perhaps a fort, annexe, *vicus* or an industrial complex" (Leary, this volume).

The second aspect is the circumstantial but convincing evidence for pottery production close to the excavated site. Of the non-samian and non-mortarium pottery many sherds were soft, indicating underfiring, and some were burnt. These features suggest that some of the vessels from which they came were 'wasters' ('seconds'), i.e. misfired examples that would normally be disposed of or used locally to the kilns but would not be deemed suitable for trade. In addition, the actual fabrics of a number of different types of pottery are very similar to one another - many of the vessels seem to be made of the same clay. This would be a strange coincidence if the pots were purchased piecemeal and

either indicates that the pottery had a single remote, but otherwise unknown source, or that there was a potter working nearby. Much the same factors specifically apply to the mortaria (a particularly well studied and understood sub-set of Roman pottery) with the eight to eleven vessels from this phase being produced of a previously unknown fabric in Flavian-Trajanic forms generally dated up to 120 AD. It is further suggestive that there are no mortaria sherds from any other known source present. None of the sherds exhibited any use-wear, one was broken in the kiln and another overfired, characteristics that again suggest that some or even all these vessels were wasters (Hartley, this volume), which would not have travelled far from their source.

Summing up the entire assemblage in this phase, Leary says, "the character of the assemblage indicates the nearby presence of a potter working in a wholly Roman tradition with strong Continental links with Gaul and, as such, an association with the military is certain" (Leary, this volume). As Hartley further points out in her analysis of the mortaria (this volume), the only reason that a potter would set up at Nostell would be if there was sufficient demand for his goods, which at this early date must mean a military establishment, and one located much closer than Castleford or Doncaster.

Some further support for a military connection in phase 2 is provided by other finds. The quern with opposed D-shaped hoppers found in a phase 3 context may well have been residual and its possible military association is suggestive but it is the assemblage of ceramic building material that is most interesting. Although far from conclusive, the presence of a piece of box-flue tile and fragments of *bessales* (square bricks) raise the possibility that there may have been a hypocaust heating system in a building nearby. The finds were unphased having come from undated or medieval contexts. However, given the non-military and seemingly low status nature of the material culture of later phases, any hypocaust has the highest probability of dating from this early military phase. If so, combined with the other evidence, the most likely site of a hypocaust would in fact be a bathhouse associated with a fort, although a commander's house, command building (*praetorium*) or even a *mansio* (roadside station designed primarily for Imperial couriers) cannot be ruled out. None, though, are likely to have been in the very immediate proximity of the excavated areas, or greater numbers of brick or tile fragments would have been encountered. An intriguing possibility is that the Roman building materials had been re-used in the medieval period as suggested by Tibbles (this volume), and this might point to a connection between the choice of site for the eleventh century hermitage and a putative Roman fort at Nostell (see below).

Various forts are known in the area of which Castleford is the best understood, but there were also forts at Slack, Doncaster, Roall and Burghwallis. Other forts have been postulated, with varying degrees of certainty, at Adel and Thorpe Audlin (Chadwick 2009). The relatively short period of evidence for military use (from the late first to early second century) is typical of the forts known from the region. At Castleford, a fort was established in the early 70s AD and abandoned for a short time in 86 AD before a second phase of occupation from around 90 to 100 AD (Abramson, Berg and Fossick 1999). The fort at Slack appears to have been decommissioned in around 140 AD (Chadwick 2009) and the original fort at Doncaster was decommissioned around 120 AD, although it was subsequently rebuilt on a smaller scale in around 160 (Buckland and Magilton 1986).

In contrast to the evidence of the pottery and other artefacts, there is no specifically military form to the excavated features at Nostell. Although various cut features from the excavation are dated to this period, none take forms of the sort expected from the defences or the characteristic internal buildings and infrastructure of a Roman fort. Only the large ditch [1220] in the access road approaches the scale expected from the defences of a fort or fort annexe but there seems little doubt of its pre-Roman date. There is a Romano-British re-cut at the top of the ditch [1251], securely dated by the very early Roman assemblage of pottery found in its primary fill, but at a maximum of 1.25 metres deep it does not seem to be large enough to be a clear example of a defensive ditch. A more serious problem is that only a six metre length of it was found in the access road. As there is no sign of a continuation into the main car park excavation, or any sign of a return in the rest of the access road to the west or the evaluation trenches to the east, it probably terminated in the unexcavated area between the car park and the access road and thus did not form a defensive circuit. It is just possible, though it would be bad luck given the scale of the trenches, that either the access road excavation to the west or evaluation trenches to the east fell in an entrance in a circuit ditch, thus displaying no sign of a continuation of the ditch. If it did, though, it would notably have been sited well down the slope of the ridge, on militarily disadvantageous ground, separated from the line of the speculated Roman road. The interpretation of the re-cut is ambiguous but it is unlikely to be evidence of military defences.

Instead of a fort *per se*, the excavations have uncovered remains of extra-mural activity. Castleford, Roall and Slack had associated *vici* (small civilian settlements close to and subordinate to the fort) and annexes (extensions to the fort with their own defences and used for metal working, stabling and bathhouses), which is more likely to be the kind of activity so far revealed at Nostell. However, in comparison with the well-studied example of the *vicus* at Castleford, the layout of the site does not fit particularly well with what might have been expected. At Castleford the *vicus* was established in the early 70s, at the same time as the first fort was organised, on a grid pattern aligned north-south and east-west. The plot boundaries were defined by ditches, gullies and wooden drains with metalled tracks between some of the plots and buildings (Abramson and Fossick 1999). The only evidence for organised boundaries at Nostell that would echo such a pattern were the three shallow ditches in the southwest part of the main car park (ditches [1201], [1203/1383] and [1010/1018/1024/1055/1057] but these did not continue across the rest of the site and there is no sign of intensive occupation within their bounds. There was a considerable degree of variation in the character of different *vici*, and it has been suggested that the Castleford example is exceptional in having been specifically laid out in a planned grid pattern rather than developing piecemeal (Dearne 1991), but it remains true that the concentration of buildings and occupation that would be expected in a *vicus* is absent at Nostell.

If the Nostell site does represent part of an extra-mural settlement, it may have been on the fringe of a more organised area. This may have been on the edge of a *vicus*, or a more dispersed area of activity such as the industrial area found at Derby

Racecourse (Dool 1985). This consisted of a discrete area of industrial activity, principally pottery production, with several examples of kilns and six wells that was less intensively occupied than a *vicus*. It lay on the approach road to the fort at Derby but was around 700m from the fort itself and beyond the putative *vicus*, which lay immediately outside the entrance to the fort. Although it might be tempting to see a direct parallel here, given the evidence in the pottery assemblage for nearby pottery kilns in this phase, no actual kilns have yet been found at Nostell. The geophysical survey carried out as part of the evaluation did not pick up any of the characteristic signals given out by kilns (although, surprisingly, neither did it detect the heavily fired oven [1639]). However, the physical scope of the geophysical survey was limited and it may be that further, more wide-ranging geophysical survey in the future may locate the kiln(s) at Nostell.

The idea of an extra-mural settlement that is more remote from a fort than a *vicus* is perhaps supported by the nature of the assemblage samian pottery. Not only were there relatively few sherds of samian from the first and early second centuries compared with what might be expected from a military establishment, but the absence of cups and decorated vessels contrasts with the far more diverse range of samian forms in the first two phases of Castleford fort (Monteil, this volume). This indicates that, whatever else was going on at this site in phase 2, the evidence for fine Romanised dining is limited. This aspect of the pottery assemblage as a whole has a non-residential character, which fits with the notion that this site may be of a more industrial nature.

The other features from this phase include a well [1160], two successive clay-lined pit/cisterns [1603] and [1168], a possible posthole structure close to the well, an oven [1639] that probably dates to this phase, a group of postholes on the eastern edge of the main excavation area that may form part of a building extending beyond the limit of excavation and other occasional pits and postholes. Although the well and clay-lined pits/cisterns, the oven and the new boundaries indicate a significant degree of organisation and hint at a specific but indeterminate function or functions their character does not, either singly or collectively, belong exclusively to a military site, nor are they characteristic of any

other identifiable site form. The well is a general feature and, given the unknown function of the clay-lined pits and the domestic or agricultural role of the oven, there is nothing specifically military about them, although all might have been present in a *vicus* attached to a fort.

The remains at Nostell are, though, uncharacteristic of other recognised types of military related sites. A number of Roman camps are known across Yorkshire (Welfare and Swan 1995, Ottaway 2003), but the only nearby example is at Jaw Hill, Kirkhamgate (Esmonde Cleary 1997) just to the northwest of Wakefield. It is not likely that a Roman camp – by definition a temporary establishment even if seasonally occupied (Welfare and Swan 1995) – would support pottery kilns or a substantial stone-cut oven and stone-lined well. The proximity of the proposed Roman road on the line of the A638 may suggest the presence of a *mansio* (a roadside station designed primarily for Imperial couriers). Little is known about *mansiones* in the north of England (Faull and Moorhouse 1981). The only Yorkshire example identified with any certainty is some way distant at Catterick, where the *mansio* (consisting of several buildings on a 0.5ha site) was constructed next to Dere Street. It was built shortly after the abandonment of the first fort in around 120 and was demolished in late second or early third century (Burnham and Wacher 1990) and therefore post-dated the military remains at Nostell. However, it is hard to see how a *mansio* would have required a potter-in-residence (unless, as suggested by Faull and Moorhouse, the facility developed into a village or small town; highly unlikely at this early date) although the need for a food processing/baking related feature like the oven might be more in keeping.

As mentioned in the introduction, it has been previously proposed that the A638, which runs past the southern boundary of the site, may have originated as a Roman road - an extension of Margary road 721 from Bradford to join with the Doncaster to Castleford road (Margary 1973, road 28b). When it was made this suggestion was based solely on a logical extension of a known road, without physical evidence to support it, and was not accepted by Margary (1973) or the West Yorkshire Archaeological Survey (Faull and Moorhouse 1981). However the subsequent discovery of the Roman camp at

Kirkhamgate and the present discovery at Nostell of what appears to be a military site on the projected line of the road now offer significant support to the suggestion. Although not all Roman camps need to have been 'marching camps' (Welfare and Swan 1995), built to accommodate troops on the move, it is nonetheless quite likely that Kirkhamgate was built next to a road or at least an established route. Forts (more permanent establishments than camps) though are almost always next to roads (a rare exception being Roall which is believed to have been supplied by river) and the military presence suggested by the discoveries at Nostell would thus seem to confirm the presence of a Roman road. Although its original form is not known, the road must have crossed the watercourse that now forms the Upper, Middle and Lower Lakes to the west of the mansion. The ford or bridge would have naturally been a point of strategic importance and may point to the reason that a military establishment was sited at Nostell.

Phases 3-5. *Rural settlement from the mid second to fourth centuries*

The ceramic evidence indicates a major change in the nature of occupation on the site after the mid second century, becoming characteristically typical of contemporary rural settlement. There was a change both in the forms of the pottery (no flagons, cups and only a single beaker) and in its sources, with no 'local' fabrics as found in phase 2. So profound is the shift that Leary (this volume) goes so far as to suggest that the site may have been temporarily abandoned , "in this phase the fabrics found in phase 2 are only present as residual sherds and there appears to be a complete change in the source of the pottery as well as the types being used. It is possible that there was a hiatus in occupation in the early second century." However, an anomalous exception to this general pattern comes when local production of mortaria recommences in the later part of the period, after a gap of around two hundred years. Sherds were found from three vessels in the typical shapes of Mancetter-Hartshill mortaria, but made from a previously unknown clay source the same or similar to the kind used in the 'local' phase 2 pottery (presumably a small isolated deposit of clay in the vicinity of Nostell). Although there was no evidence – such as clear deposits of wasters or kilns themselves - it seems that mortaria were again

being produced at or near the site in the late third or early fourth century by a potter or potters who had moved here from the main production centres in the Midlands (Hartley, this volume). Further fieldwork beyond the limits of the site might, relatively easily, be able to identify the location of the production site, and very probably, that previously established for the benefit the military.

In phase 3 a number of ditched boundaries appeared in the southwestern part of the site as well as the beginnings of pit digging nearby that would continue throughout the rest of Romano-British occupation. There was nothing to indicate the original purpose of the pits but in several cases the quantity of broken pottery in their fills suggests that they ended their lives as refuse pits. Also in this phase, a corn-drier and an associated posthole structure was constructed in the access road area, seemingly deliberately isolated from other features – as was not uncommon, avoiding the risk of fire in domestic areas. A rectangular posthole structure was built north of the refuse pits and a group of postholes in the east part of the car park may also have been a structure (although only one of the postholes was clearly dated to this phase and the pattern of any putative structure was not clear). Concentration of activity in the southwest corner of the site seems to continue the emphasis on this area established by the phase 2 boundary ditches. In addition, ditch [1008/1014], established in phase 3, appeared to respect the former phase 2 ditch [1010/1018/1024/1055/1057], despite the latter being backfilled (perhaps indicating that a bank and/or hedge remained) and the very upper part of the terminal of ditch [1203/1383] appears to have still been open. Despite abrupt change in the nature of the pottery, there appears to have been some continuity in the layout of land boundaries during this phase.

In phase 4, in contrast to earlier phases, there do not appear to have been any ditched boundaries in use (although the imprecision of the pottery dating means that some or all of the small-scale boundaries assigned to phase 5 may have been backfilled in the later third century and thus may have been still open and used in the early third century). However, the pattern of pit use in the southwest corner of the site established in the previous phase continued with seven pits containing finds from this phase in their backfills.

In phase 5 there were three pits in the southwest corner of the site and new boundaries made up of short sections of ditch (ditches [1145], [1119] and [1071/1085/1100/1195]) with postholes in the south central part of the main car park area. These boundaries are dated only by pottery in their fills and it is possible that the stratigraphically earlier L-shaped ditches that appear to form an entrance (with two associated postholes) may date from phase 4 or before and were only backfilled in this phase. The artefactual evidence indicates a possible intensification of activity in the late third and early fourth century. It is from this phase that there is more evidence for smithing, although this must be treated cautiously as the smithing hearth bottoms and slag of the type found are long lived artefacts and could easily be residual. It is also from this phase that, as mentioned above, there is good evidence that mortaria were being produced at or near the site, although the evidence does not suggest production of other kinds of pottery.

Because of the limitations of the excavated area, it is difficult to understand the relationship of the revealed boundaries to a wider landscape and therefore to assess their role. With the one exception of the large ditch [1220] in the access road, most of the boundaries were relatively small and shallow. At the mid second to mid fourth century Romano-British rural settlement at Thurnscoe in South Yorkshire (Neal and Fraser 2004), 15km south of Nostell, the earliest phase of two rectangular enclosures was defined by relatively shallow U-shaped enclosure ditches of an average of 0.6-0.7 metres wide and 0.35-0.4 metres deep, which is a similar scale to the Nostell boundaries. In contrast, the much larger pair of enclosures in phase 2 and 3 of the site was defined by broader and deeper (2m wide and 1m deep) ditches. It is therefore possible that the boundaries may relate to a settlement analogous to Thurnscoe phase 1, but on the basis of the present excavation it is not possible to say more about the nature of the settlement, or even whether it was enclosed by an undiscovered boundary ditch or open in nature.

Although several postholes occurring singly and in groups were found in phases 3 to 5 at Nostell,

there was no direct evidence of domestic buildings in the form of roundhouses, hearths or even the posthole 'arcs' that are the best candidates for dwellings at Thurnscoe. Instead, where it was possible to deduce the shape of buildings these had the character of rectangular lightweight structures and may have related to agricultural activity, as was the case with the posthole cluster adjacent to corn-drier [1265]. As far as pinpointing the location of any dwellings is concerned, it is possible that the pits in the southwest corner of the site, which appear to have been filled with rubbish, may have lain close to a domestic area sited beyond the excavation to the southwest.

The discovery of this Romano-British agricultural settlement is given context by the nearby cropmark evidence and the findings of other small excavations within the estate (Figure 25). Cropmarks shown on an aerial photograph revealed part of a rectangular enclosure, a possible roundhouse, and a series of other ditches. This area of cropmarks lies either side of the approach to the house, 30 metres east-northeast of the entrance to the stable block and just over 100 metres southeast of the mansion itself. The full site extent not visible, as the parching was limited in extent (NAA 2001, 31). That the remains were wider in extent than shown by the cropmarks was confirmed by the discovery of further ditches with small amounts of Roman pottery in two small excavations, one beneath the 'refectory' (OSA 2008c) and one across the vista to the west of the mansion (OSA 2008a). A watching brief during refurbishment of the stable block in 2010 revealed an undated pit in the courtyard and an undated ditch in an electric cable trench linking the stable block and the new visitor car park (OSA forthcoming). The lakes to the west, although much altered in the monastic and post medieval period, and Hardwick Beck to the north may have been in similar positions, forming the natural boundaries of this particular field system. It is possible that the field system was directly related to the settlement evidence uncovered in the car park excavations, but where they have been excavated the features associated with the field system contained either no pottery, or pottery too crude and poorly preserved to be dated with any certainty, meaning that the chronological relationship has yet to be firmly established.

Further afield, two other cropmark enclosure sites have been found just outside the estate. The northern one (West Yorkshire Historic Environment Record (WY HER) reference 789) lies approximately 320 metres north of Obelisk Lodge, which is sited at the northernmost point of the National Trust estate boundary. The southern cropmarks, (WY HER reference 786), lie approximately 450 metres south of Wragby Lodge. They too may be associated with settlement in phases 3-5 of the Nostell car park excavation and, if this could be demonstrated, it would point to the existence of an extensive Romano-British farming landscape in the mid second to fourth centuries. However, no dating evidence has been recovered from the sites of these other cropmarks and it remains possible that they may date to the early or pre-Roman period.

Agricultural structures

Four-post structures

Two four-post structures were present in the northern part of the main car park. These common features are usually interpreted as granaries with raised floors to aid air circulation in order to minimize the risk of fire associated with stored grain, and to protect against rodents and rising damp. In some cases the presence of charred grain in the postholes seems to confirm the purpose of the structures as at Castle Hills site M near Garforth (Brown et al. 2007) and Sutton Common (Van de Noort 2007), although no such evidence was present at Nostell. (Chadwick (2009) has suggested that the burnt grain is not accidental loss, but deliberate deposition - perhaps an 'offering' of some kind – into the postholes at the time of construction. At Nostell two postholes were found next to the southwest corner of one of the granaries. Adjacent postholes of this

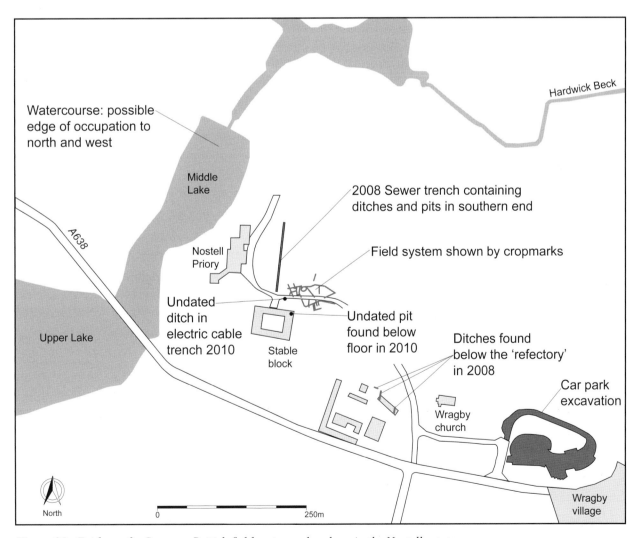

Figure 25. Evidence for Romano-British field systems elsewhere in the Nostell estate

81

sort have been interpreted as the bases of ladders consisting of a single upright shaft with projecting rungs on either side (e.g. Van de Noort 2007).

Examples of four-post granaries are relatively common on Iron Age sites in the region. At Castle Hills Site M near Garforth at least 15 were found associated with Iron Age settlement and the charred grain from one of the postholes was dated to 390-180 cal BC (Druce 2007). At the Iron Age 'marsh fort' of Sutton Common near Doncaster there were an extraordinary 115-155 four-post structures (Van de Noort 2007), often arranged in rows of 6 set 1.5m apart (a similar distance apart as the Nostell examples). At least two examples were found in the Iron Age phase at Dalton Parlours (Wrathmell and Nicholson 1990).

However, four-post structures are also occasionally known from Romano-British period sites. In what was at the time her definitive study, Morris lists a handful of examples in the south of England (Morris 1979) and examples are known in Yorkshire from Swillington Common (Chadwick 2009), where a radiocarbon date of 85-385 cal AD was obtained, and phase 2 (second century AD) of Welton Villa in the East Riding (Mackey 1999). So, although the balance of probabilities favours a pre-Roman Iron Age date, this is not certain.

Oven and corn-drier

Two agricultural or domestic heating structures were found, an oven and a corn-drier, both exhibiting burnt grain in their fills. The oven [1639] was dated by radiocarbon to 70 – 230 Cal.AD with a 95% probability and between 80 and 140 Cal.AD with a 68% probability. The grain assemblage found in its firing chamber was consistent with its use in food preparation or the parching of cereal grains as a first step in milling. The corn-drier [1265] was more securely dated to the second half of the second century. Both features were poorly preserved and in neither case did a superstructure survive.

Oven [1639] was circular with two adjacent fire boxes exhibiting the scorching associated with high temperatures. The pattern of heat distribution shown by the heat-affected bedrock suggested that the two circular cuts functioned as the fire-boxes heating a now absent superstructure (or pair of

superstructures), while the larger oval cut was the 'draw hole' or stoking area, used for both raking out ashes from the fire box and for loading fresh fuel. Analysis of the cereal grains concluded that they were, "… likely to have been charred accidentally during food preparation or parching" (Simmons, this volume), which fits with the use of the feature as a 'domestic' oven used in food preparation.

A curious aspect of the oven was the lack of evidence for a building around or near the feature, as might be expected for a domestic oven. There is, though, a precedent for this as uncovered bread ovens are a common feature of Roman forts (such as at Duone fort in Stirling, Moloney 1999), where they tend to be built into the rear of the rampart. In this case it is possible that there was a building with ephemeral foundations, of which no trace now survives, but it is also a possibility that this was not a 'domestic' oven for bread making or similar duties. The double firebox does not have any precise parallels in the region. At Castleford there are several superficially similar clay-built 'double ovens' in the *vicus* but they seem to have functioned differently with an external fire heating two clay chambers via a short flue, rather than the two chambers functioning as fireboxes (Abramson and Fossick 1999). The lack of any finds in the backfill and use-deposits probably rules out an industrial function like pottery or ironworking. The burnt grain assemblage would be consistent with the parching of cereal grains, carried out to enable easier milling (van der Veen 1989). However, if the oven did fulfill this role, its form is very different from the corn-driers normally used for the task. In particular, it seems to lack any facility for heating a raised drying floor, which is normally achieved by excavating a wide pit or narrower flue or flue system to direct hot air below a wooden floor.

The basic elements of corn-driers were a suspended or raised wooden floor above a flue channelling air heated by a fire in a 'fire box' area, fed with fuel via a 'draw hole' (through which ash could also be removed). The aim was to keep the fire remote from the wooden drying floor while at the same time using the hot air to gently heat the grain by means of various designs of flues and baffles. Corn-drier [1265] did not accord to the classic T-shaped layout described by Morris (1979), shared by some corn-driers excavated in the region such as at Womersley

(Buckland and Dolby 1987), Thurnscoe (Neal and Fraser 2004), Wattle Syke (Chadwick 2009) and several of the examples at Dalton Parlours (Wrathmell and Nicholson 1990). However forms and construction techniques vary widely and many different shapes have also been excavated in the region as with the rectangular form at Ferrybridge (Roberts 2005, Figure 102), three different examples at Pontefract with a straight flue, a rectangular and circular type (Turner 1987), and straight-flued types at Dalton Parlours (Wrathmell and Nicholson 1990) and a possible straight flued example at Thurnscoe (Neal and Fraser 2004, flue 1134). Further afield, an unusual and elaborately designed example comprising a double layered wattle dome covered with fired clay found at Melton in the East Riding (Fenton-Thomas 2011) demonstrates the wide range of possible forms.

Corn-drier [1265] is a variation on more familiar straight flue types, except that in this case a single fire box served two opposing flues, lined with sandstone flags bonded with clay. Between the open ends of the two channels was an ashy deposit, presumed to include the remains from the final firing of the structure. This contained substantial quantities of well-preserved cereal grains, identified as spelt wheat, free threshing wheat and hulled barley and spelt wheat chaff (Simmons, this volume). It was not fully clear where the draw hole lay, but it is probable that the ill-defined projecting cut on the west side of the feature was the place from where the fire, towards the east of the feature, was tended. There was evidence for a post built structure around the corn-drier although whether this was a lightweight roofed building, wind-break or even part of the superstructure supporting the actual drying floor(s) is unclear. The large, well-preserved second century corn-drier at Ferrybridge also included several associated postholes suggesting a surrounding structure (Roberts 2005). This corn-drier seems to have been in a relatively isolated position as if deliberately sited at some distance from other activities, as has been suggested for the corn-driers at Apple Tree Close, Pontefract (Turner 1987).

Burial

A number of possible undated burial features were found. All of these features are located in the southeastern part of the main car park, probably a peripheral area in all phases. The main difficulty in assessing the evidence was a total lack of bone preservation, confirmed by a similar absence of animal bone in the excavated features of the site. It is likely that the graves once contained burials. Poor bone preservation has been noted on other sites located on the Coal Measures sandstones, such as Iron Age and Romano-British settlement at Bullerthorpe Lane, north of Swillington and Iron Age occupation at Manor Farm, north of Garforth (Roberts, Burgess & Berg 2001). Several grave-shaped features excavated on Coal Measures sandstone bedrock at the Romano-British settlement at Thurnscoe, west of Doncaster were all devoid of bone (Neal and Fraser 2004) and similar possible 'empty' graves were found at Methley, near Castleford (MAP cited in Chadwick 2009), also on Coal Measures sandstone. By contrast similar types of site located on Lower Magnesian Limestone bedrock, such as Parlington Hollins and Ferrybridge, contain representative examples of numerous domesticated and wild animal species and well-preserved human inhumation burials (Roberts 2005).

Features [1277] and [1317] were the correct shape to be grave cuts. They were rectangular with lengths of 1.85 and 1.7 metres and widths of 0.7 and 0.8 metres respectively; both were 0.3 metres deep. At Thurnscoe, at least twenty one grave-shaped pits were excavated and most were strikingly similar in dimensions to the two Nostell examples. They were interpreted by the excavators as graves from which the bones had degraded in the acid soil (Neal and Fraser 2004). None of the Thurnscoe 'graves' contained bone and only one contained grave goods in the form of a South Yorkshire Late Roman Redware bowl (imitating a samian form) that dated to 240 AD or later. The graves were thought to date from all phases of the settlement from second to fourth centuries.

A further probable grave, close to the other two, was rectangular and measured 1.4 metres long, 0.5 metres wide and had a maximum depth of 0.2 metres. The edges of this grave were lined with vertically set sandstone slabs while more broken sandstone rubble on the northwest side of the cut may be the plough damaged capping, or the remains of the base of a cairn. Late-Roman or sub-Roman examples of stone-lined graves have been excavated at Parlington Hollins (see Roberts, Burgess & Berg 2001), and Romano-British examples are known from Wattle Syke, near Wetherby (Chadwick 2009). The size of the "grave" suggests that it was likely to have been for a child if the inhumation was extended, in line with the usual practice of Romano-British period burials in the region (Chadwick 2009).

Close to the grave features (grave [1317] was less than a metre away) was a ring ditch [1134] with a central pit, and with two postholes cutting the backfilled ditch together with a further posthole forming an arc. No datable material was found in association with these features. If the central oval pit was a grave it would have been of a suitable size only for a flexed or crouched burial unless it was for a child. If this feature is interpreted as the remains of a burial mound, then in form it would most likely to date to the early Bronze Age (Vyner 2008) as round barrows are very rare in Iron Age or Romano-British contexts, especially in northern England, and tend to be much larger (Brown 1977). Bronze Age barrows are known from lowland contexts in West Yorkshire at Ferrybridge, Ferry Fryston, Stanbury, and Manor Farm near Garforth (Vyner 2008). However the lack of any other material uncovered in the excavation dating to the Bronze Age, and the close physical association of the ring ditch to the presumably Romano-British 'burials', prompts a possible alternative interpretation.

Two Roman period ring ditches in the region (distinguished from roundhouse gullies principally by the absence of entrances) have been suggested as possible shrines (Chadwick 2009). At Topham Farm, Sykehouse a 12m unbroken ring gully was replaced by a 5.5 metre diameter version with two postholes within the gully (Roberts 2003). At Wattle Syke a 5m wide sub-octagonal 'ring gully' also had two postholes and a Roman coin had been placed under a rock in the base of the gully prior to backfilling (Chadwick 2009). Although the Nostell ring ditch is smaller (with a diameter of 3 metres) it does have two – possibly three – associated postholes like Sykehouse and Wattle Syke although in this case they were shown to have been dug after the infilling of the gully. The other examples had no associated burial, but the central pit at Nostell need not have been a grave but could have been a pit for the deposition of offerings. It is therefore tempting to tentatively suggest that the Nostell ring gully may be a further example of a Roman shrine.

In the context of a discussion of burials, the near-complete Roman handled jar of South Yorkshire type found during the initial trial trenching should be mentioned. It had been carefully placed upright in a man-made 'scoop' in the natural ground surface approximately 10m north east of stone-lined grave [1122]. There was no direct evidence that the vessel was related to the burials and nothing was found within the pot but it is possible that it once held a mortuary-related offerings or votive deposits. This would explain the otherwise enigmatic presence of a complete vessel, deliberately placed in an upright position.

The medieval period

Although this report has not dealt with the medieval period at Nostell Priory, the Roman bricks found in a medieval ditch to the northwest of Wragby church during the construction of the footpath to the car park have raised the possibility that Roman building materials were re-used in the medieval period (Tibbles, this volume). This in turn highlights the potential of a direct link between the discoveries from the Roman period and the poorly known history of the foundation of Nostell Priory and its hermitage predecessor. It is well-established that early Christians from the seventh century to the tenth century, and probably later as well, deliberately sited their churches and other religious institutions on top of and adjacent to Roman structures, particularly at the sites of villas, mausoleums, graveyards and, most relevant for Nostell, at military sites (Bell 1998, Bell 2005, Morris 1989). The definitive study on the subject records 256 Anglo-Saxon churches directly associated with Roman structures (Bell 2005). Not only were there good practical reasons for this (building materials, established drainage, springs, cleared sites and commanding positions over the surrounding landscape), but the sixth century Pope Gregory I seems to have deliberately associated the early Christian church with the past glory of the Roman empire, "*Roman* was largely considered synonymous with *Christian*. This association appears to be one of design rather than coincidence" (Bell 1998, 6). Among other examples known from historical documents Gregory's missionary to England, Saint Augustine, founded his first church (now Canterbury cathedral) in 597AD in what was at that time a ruined Roman town on the site of a supposed Roman church, according to Bede's *Historia Ecclesiastica* (Bede [1907], Book 1, Chapter xxxiii).

This tradition was very influential in later Christian thinking and it may be that it guided the early twelfth century - or perhaps eleventh century (NAA 2001, Frost 2007) - hermits to choose this location as the site of their hermitage. A persistent tradition locates this hermitage on the site of or near the later Wragby Church, in other words to the east of the ultimate site of the priory, although this is contradicted by the text of a grant from 1121, which suggests that the original site was to the south (Newman 2006, NAA 2001). According to the medieval Nostell Act Book, a transcription of which is held by the Nostell Estate, Wragby parish church was erected on the site of the 'old place', interpreted to mean the original site of the priory and therefore a possible site of the earlier hermitage. The 'old place' was definitely consecrated since documents indicate that it, rather than their own Priory church, was the preferred burial place of a number of the Priors. However, there is not yet any physical evidence to support this link and the association between the church and the 'old place' has been questioned (NAA 2001, 33). Much remains to be established, but it is possible to conjecture that when the location of the Roman establishment is found, it is likely to have had at least one masonry building, and the original hermitage may be found too.

4.2 Concluding remarks

Investigations at the site of the new visitor car park have provided the vast majority of archaeologically excavated information for the Iron Age and Romano-British periods at Nostell. The work significantly enhanced and put into context the smaller scale discoveries from these periods made over the past decade, on both National Trust property and that still owned by Lord St Oswald. Although five phases of activity have been indicated, ranging from the pre-Roman Iron Age to the fourth century, for the site as a whole it remains difficult to characterise the precise nature of the occupation. In each phase, despite the presence of boundary ditches, pits, postholes and other features, the actual locus of occupation – in the form of roundhouses, barrack blocks or other kinds of dwelling – appears to have lain beyond the excavated area. The site(s) of occupation may have been very close by, and what clues there are point to the north in the case of the putative pre-Roman Iron Age phase and the southwest in the case of the later Romano-British phases. The site of the pottery production inferred from the assemblage of phase 2 pottery recovered (and again in the late third to early fourth centuries) is likely to have been close to a clay source although at present it is not certain where this may have been. Wider landscape study may locate this, and geophysical survey may find the site of the kiln or kilns.

Uncertainty about what lies beyond the site boundary is no more apparent than when considering the early Romano-British (or perhaps, more correctly, the *Roman*) phase 2, of the late first to early second centuries. It is clearly apparent from the nature of the pottery and other finds in this phase that the site was connected with the Roman military, and it is very likely that a hitherto unknown fort stood in the vicinity. There is, however, no corresponding convincing trace of recognisably military structure in the excavated features. The best that can be said is that the boundary ditches, well, clay-lined pits, oven and scattered postholes of this phase are far from native British in character and could belong to the fringes of a civilian settlement (*vicus*) lying next to a fort, a more dispersed industrial area linked with a fort but lying less close to it than a *vicus*, or – less likely – a facility for imperial couriers (*mansio*).

A Roman military and/or administrative presence at Nostell would add significantly to our picture of the Roman conquest and occupation of West Yorkshire, not least seeming to confirm the Roman origins of the present A638, linking the fort at Doncaster with Elslack fort via both Nostell and the temporary camp at Jaw Hill, Kirkhamgate. It raises, too, the possibility that the early Christian hermits may have deliberately sited their community at a Roman site, an intriguing potential link between the discoveries reported in this book and the later history of the medieval priory. Full confirmation of the presence of any fort must await further fieldwork in the area. What is certain is that the new visitor car park has dramatically shifted our understanding of the pre-monastic history of the estate and has, for the first time, brought the Romans of Nostell, and Wragby's first industry – pottery production - firmly into view.

Bibliography

Published sources

Annable, K. 1960. *The Romano-British Pottery at Cantley Housing Estate, Doncaster.* (Doncaster: Doncaster Museums Publication XXIV)

Abramson, P. and Fossick, M. 1999. 'The major trenches: excavations of the vicus, 1974 and 1980-82.' In Abramson, P., Berg, D. and Fossick, M. *Roman Castleford Excavations 1974-85. Volume II: the Structural and Environmental Evidence.* (Leeds: Yorkshire Archaeology 5) 126-151

Abramson, P., Berg, D. and Fossick, M. 1999. *Roman Castleford Excavations 1974-85. Volume II: the Structural and Environmental Evidence.* (Leeds: Yorkshire Archaeology 5)

Bastow, M. 1999. 'The botanical material.' In P. Abramson, D.S. Berg and M.R. Fossick (eds.) *Roman Castleford excavations 1974-85. Volume II: The Structural and Environmental Evidence.* (Leeds: Yorkshire Archaeology 5), 163- 222

Bede [translated by Sellar, A. 1907]. *Ecclesiastical History of England.* (London: George Bell and Sons)

de la Bédoyère, G. 1991. *The Buildings of Roman Britain* (London: Batsford Ltd)

Bell, A. and Evans, J. 2002. 'Pottery from the CFA excavations.' In Wilson, P. (ed.) *Cataractonium: Roman Catterick and its hinterland: Excavations and research, 1958-1997.* (York: Council for British Archaeology Research Report 128)

Bell, T. 1998. 'Churches on Roman Buildings: Christian Associations and Roman Masonry in Anglo-Saxon England.' *Medieval Archaeology* 42, 1-18

Bell, T. 2005. *The Religious Reuse of Roman Structures in Early Medieval England.* (British Archaeological Reports, British Series 390)

Bidwell, P. and Croom, A. 2010. 'The supply and use of pottery on Hadrian's Wall in the 4th century.' In Collins, R and Allason-Jones, L. *Finds from the Frontier: Material Culture in the 4th-5th centuries.* (York: Council for British Archaeology Research Report 162) 20-36

Birss, R. 1985. 'Coarse Pottery.' In Dool et al. 'Roman Derby: Excavations 1968-1983.' *Derbyshire Archaeological Journal* 105, 90-124

Birss, R. 1986. 'The Roman Pottery.' In Branigan, K and Housley, J. and C. (1986) Two Roman Lead Pigs from Carsington. *Derbyshire Archaeological Journal* 106, 5-17

Boardman, S and Jones, G. 1990. 'Experiments on the effects of charring on cereal plant components.' *Journal of Archaeological Science* 17: 1 – 11

Brassington, M. 1971. 'A Trajanic kiln complex near Little Chester, Derby, 1968.' *Antiquaries Journal* 51, 36-69

Brassington, M. 1980. 'Derby Racecourse kiln excavations 1972-3.' *Antiquaries Journal* 60, 8-47

Brockwell, M. 1915. *Catalogue of the Pictures and other Works of Art in the Collection of Lord St Oswald at Nostell Priory.* (Princeton: Constable)

Brodribb, G. 1987. *Roman Brick and Tile* (Gloucester: Alan Sutton Publishing)

Brown, A. 1977. `The Roman barrow cemetery on Borough Hill, Daventry'. In *Northamptonshire Archaeology* 12, 185-90

Brown, F., Howard-Davies, C., Brennand, M., Boyle, A., Evans, T., O'Connor, S., Spence, A., Heawood, R. and Lupton, A. 2007. *The Archaeology of the A1(M) Darrington to Dishforth DBFO Road Scheme.* (Lancaster: Lancaster Imprints)

Buckland, P. and Dolby, M. 1987. 'A Roman site at Womersley'. *Yorkshire Archaeological Journal* 59: 1-8

Buckland, P., Dolby, M. and Magilton, J. 1980. 'The Romano-British pottery industries of South Yorkshire: a review' *Britannia* 11, 145-64

Buckland, P. and Magilton, J.R. 1986. *The Archaeology of Doncaster 1: The Roman Civil Settlement.* (British Archaeological Reports, British Series 148)

Buckley, D. and Major, H. 1990. 'Quernstones'. In Wrathmell, S and Nicholson, A. *Dalton Parlours: Iron Age Settlement and Roman Villa* (Leeds: Yorkshire Archaeology 3)

Buckley, D. and Major, H. 1998. 'The Quernstones.' In Cool, H. and Philo, C. (eds.) *Roman Castleford: Excavations 1974-85, Volume 1: The Small Finds* (Leeds: Yorkshire Archaeology 4)

Burnham, B. and Wacher, J. 1990. *Small Towns of Roman Britain.* (Berkerley: University of California Press)

Burton, J. 1785. *Monasticon Eboracense and the Ecclesiastical History of Yorkshire.* (York: N. Nickson) 329–40

Dark, P. 1999. 'Pollen evidence for the environment of Roman Britain.' *Britannia* 30: 247-272

Darling, M. 2004. 'Guidelines for the archiving of Roman pottery.' *Journal of Roman Pottery Studies* 11, 67-75

Davies, B., Richardson, B. and Tomber, R. 1994. *A Dated Corpus of Early Roman Pottery from the City of London.* (York: Council for British Archaeology Research Report 98)

Dearne, M. 1991. 'The Military Vici of the South Pennines: Retrospect and Prospect.' In Hodges, R. and Smith, K (eds) *Recent Developments in the Archaeology of the Peak District* (Sheffield: J R Collis Publications)

Dickinson, B. and Hartley, B. 2000. 'The samian.' In Rush, P., Dickinson, B., Hartley B and Hartley, K. *Roman Castleford Excavations 1974-85 Volume III: The Pottery* (Leeds: Yorkshire Archaeology 6) 5-88

Dool, J. 1985. 'Derby Racecourse: Excavations on the Roman Industrial Settlement, 1974.' *Derbyshire Archaeological Journal* 105, 155-183

Dore, J. 2005. 'The Roman pottery.' In Bishop, M., Allen, D., Boghi, F., Brickstock, R., Coulston, J., Dickinson, B., Dodge, H., Dore, J., van Driel-

Murray, C., Gidney, L., Hartley, K., Huntley, J., McDonnell, G., MacLean, P., Padley, T., 'A New Flavian Military Site at Roecliffe, North Yorkshire' *Britannia* 36: 164-174

Druce, D. 2007. 'The Plant Remains.' In Brown et al. 2007

English Heritage. 1991. *Management of Archaeological Projects* (London: HBMC)

English Heritage. 2008. *Geophysical Survey in Archaeological Field Evaluation* (Swindon: English Heritage Publishing)

Esmonde Cleary, A. 1998. 'Roman Britain in 1997.' *Britannia* 29: 388

Esmonde Cleary, A. 1997. 'Roman Britain in 1996.' *Britannia* 28: 420-1

Evans, J. 1993. 'Pottery function and finewares in the Roman north.' *Journal of Roman Pottery Studies* 6, 95-119

Evans, J. 2001a. 'Material approaches to the identification of different Romano-British site types.' In James, S and Millett, M. *Britons and Romans: advancing an archaeological agenda*, 26-35 (York: Council for British Archaeology Research Report 125)

Evans, J. 2001b. 'Roman pottery.' In Roberts, I., Burgess A. and Berg, D. (eds.) *A New Link to the Past. The Archaeological Landscape of the M1-A1 Link Road.* (Leeds: Yorkshire Archaeology 7)

Evans, J. 2004. 'Roman pottery.' In Burgess, A. and Roberts, I. *Two Late Iron Age/Romano-British Settlement Sites near Whitwood, West Yorkshire.* (Wakefield: Archaeological Services (WYAS) Publications 6)

Faull, M. and Moorhouse, S (eds). 1981. *West Yorkshire : an archaeological survey to A.D. 1500.* (Wakefield: West Yorkshire MCC)

Fenton-Thomas, C. 2009. *A Place By the Sea: Excavations at Sewerby Cottage Farm, Bridlington.* (York: On-Site Archaeology Monograph 1)

Fenton-Thomas, C. 2011. *Where Sky and Yorkshire and Water Meet: The story of the Melton landscape from prehistory to the present.* (York: On-Site Archaeology Monograph 2)

Frost, J. 2007. *The Foundation of Nostell Priory 1109-1153* (York: Borthwick Institute Papers 111)

Bibliography

Gale, R. 2004. 'The charred wood.' In Neal, P and Fraser, R (eds.) 'A Romano-British enclosed farmstead at Billingley Drive, Thurnscoe, South Yorkshire.' *Yorkshire Archaeological Journal* 76: 7 – 92

Gillam, J. 1940. 'Romano-British Derbyshire ware.' *Antiquaries Journal* 19, 429-37

Gillam, J. 1976. 'Coarse fumed ware in northern Britain and beyond,' *Glasgow Archaeological Journal* 4, 57-89

Giorgi, J. 2004. 'The charred plant remains.' In Neal, P and Fraser, R (eds.) Romano-British enclosed farmstead at Billingley Drive, Thurnscoe, South Yorkshire. *Yorkshire Archaeological Journal* 76: 7 – 92

Greene, K. 1978. 'Flavian "Ring and Dot" beakers from Londinium: Verulamium Form 130 and allied types.' In Arthur, P and Marsh, G. (eds) *Early Fine Wares in Roman Britain.* (British Archaeological Reports, British series 57) 109-116

Hall, A. and Huntley, J. 2007. *A Review of the evidence for Macrofossil Plant Remains from Archaeological Deposits in Northern England. Research Department Report Series 87.* (Swindon: English Heritage)

Hartley, K. 1998. 'The incidence of stamped mortaria in the Roman Empire with special reference to imports to Britain.' in Bird, J (ed.) *Form and Fabric: studies in Rome's material past in honour of B. R. Hartley* (Oxford: Oxbow Monograph 80) 199-217

Hartley, K. and Tomber, R. 2006. 'A Mortarium Bibliography with Reference to Roman Britain (with a contribution on Wales by Peter Webster)' *Journal of Roman Pottery Studies* 13

Heslop, D. 2008. *Patterns of Quern Production, Acquisition and Deposition* (Leeds: YAS Occasional Paper 5)

Hillman, G. 1984. 'Interpretation of archaeological plant remains: the application of ethnographic models from Turkey.' In van Zeist, W and Casparie, W (eds.) *Plants and Ancient Man.* (Rotterdam: Balkema), 1 – 42

Huntley, J. 2002. 'Environmental Archaeology : Mesolithic to Roman period.' In *Past, present and future : the archaeology of Northern England : proceedings of a conference held in Durham in 1996.* Research report 5 (Durham: Architectural and Archaeological Society of Durham and Northumberland) 79-96

Leary, R. 2007. 'The Romano-British pottery.' In Brown, F., Boyle, A., Howard-Davis C. and Lupton, A. *The Archaeology of the A1 (M) Darrington to Dishforth DBFO Road Scheme* (Oxford: Oxford Archaeology Monograph) 236-254

Leary, R. 2008. 'The Iron Age and Romano-British pottery.' In Richardson, J. *The Late Iron Age and Romano-British Rural Landscape of Gunhills, Armthorpe, South Yorkshire* (Leeds: Yorkshire Archaeology 10) 25-45

Long, D. and Tipping, R. 2001. 'Roman Ridge. Pollen analysis.' In Roberts, I, Burgess, A & Berg, D (eds.) *A New Link to the Past. The Archaeological Landscape of the M1-A1 Link Road.* (Leeds: Yorkshire Archaeology 7) 225

Mackey, R. 1999. 'The Welton Villa.' In Halkon, P. (ed) *Further Light on the Parisi* Revised edition (Hull: East Riding Archaeological Society)

Margueire, D. and Hunot, J-V. 2007. 'Charcoal analysis and dendrology: data from archaeological sites in north-western France.' *Journal of Archaeological Science*, 34: 1417-1433

Margary, I. 1973. *Roman Roads in Britain* (London: John Bater)

Marsh, G. 1978. 'Early Second Century Fine Wares in the London Area.' In Arthur, P and Marsh, G. (eds) *Early Fine Wares in Roman Britain* (British Archaeological Reports British series 57) 119-223

Moloney, C. 1999. 'Duone Primary School, Duone.' In *Discovery and Excavation in Scotland* 1999, 87

Morris, P. 1979. *Agricultural Buildings in Roman Britain* (Oxford: British Archaeological Reports 70)

Morris, R. 1989. *Churches in the Landscape.* (London: Dent)

Murray, J. 1990. 'The carbonised plant remains from selected Roman deposits.' In Wrathmell,S and Nicholson, A (eds.) *Dalton Parlours. Iron Age Settlement and Roman Villa.* (Leeds: Yorkshire Archaeology 3) 189-194

Neal, P. and Fraser, R (eds.). 2004. 'A Romano-British Enclosed Farmstead At Billingley Drive, Thurnscoe, South Yorkshire.' *Yorkshire Archaeological Journal* 76: 7-92

Ottaway, P. 2003. 'The Archaeology of the Roman period in the Yorkshire Region: a Rapid Resource Assessment'. In Manby, T., Moorhouse, S. and Ottaway, P. 2003 *The Archaeology of Yorkshire: An assessment at the beginning of the 21st century* (Leeds: Yorkshire Archaeology Society)

Page, W (ed.). 1974. *A History of the County of York: Volume 3* (London: Victoria County History)

Perrin, J. 1999. 'Roman Pottery from excavations at and near to the Roman small town of Durobrivae, Water Newton, Cambridgeshire, 1956-58' *Journal of Roman Pottery Studies* 8

Phillips, H. 1973. *Edlington Wood: An ecological and archaeological survey.* (Doncaster: Doncaster Rural District Council)

Philips, J. 1950. 'A survey of the distribution of some querns of Hunsbury or allied type. In Kenyon, K Excavations at Breedon-on-the-Hill.' *Transactions of the Leicestershire Archaeological and Historical Society* 26, 75-82

Roberts, I., Burgess, A. & Berg, D (eds). 2001. *A New Link to the Past. The Archaeological Landscape of the M1-A1 Link Road.* (Leeds: Yorkshire Archaeology 7)

Roberts, I. 2003. *Excavations at Topham Farm, Sykehouse South Yorkshire. A Late Iron Age and Romano-British settlement in the Humberhead Levels* (Leeds: West Yorkshire Archaeology Service)

Roberts, I (ed.). 2005. *Ferrybridge Henge: The Ritual Landscape* (Leeds: Yorkshire Archaeology 10)

Rush, P. 2000. 'The coarse wares.' In Rush, P., Dickinson, B., Hartley B and Hartley, K. *Roman Castleford Excavations 1974-85 Volume III: The Pottery* (Leeds: Yorkshire Archaeology 6) 89-161

Rogers, G-B. 1974. 'Poteries sigillées de la Gaule centrale, I, les motifs non figurés.' In *supplément 28, GALLIA*, Paris, 1974

Rogers, G-B. 1999. *Poteries sigillées de la Gaule centrale, II, les potiers.* Two volumes, Revue archéologique SITES, Hors Série, 40

Rush, P., Dickinson, B., Hartley, B. and Hartley, K. 2000. *Roman Castleford: Excavations 1974-85. Vol. III The Pottery* (Leeds: Yorkshire Archaeology 6)

Ryan, P. 1996. *Brick in Essex from the Roman Conquest to the Reformation* (Essex: Pat Ryan)

Swan, V. 2002. 'The Roman pottery of Yorkshire in its wider historical context.' In Wilson, P. and Price, J. (eds) *Aspects of Industry in Roman Yorkshire and the North* (Oxford: Oxbow books) 35-79

Swan, V. and McBride, R. 2002. 'A Rhineland Potter at the Legionary Fortress of York.' In Aldhouse-Green, M and Webster, P (eds) *Artefacts and Archaeology Aspects of the Celtic and Roman World* (University of Wales Press) 190-233

Symonds, R. 2003. 'Romano-British amphorae.' *Journal of Roman Pottery Studies* 10, 50-59

Symonds, R. and Wade, S. 1999. *Roman pottery from excavations in Colchester, 1971-86* (Colchester: Colchester Archaeological Report 10)

Théry-Parisot, I., Chabal, L. and Chrzavzez, J. 2010. 'Anthropology and taphonomy, from wood gathering to charcoal analysis: a review of the taphonomic processes modifying charcoal assemblages, in archaeological contexts.' *Palaeogeography, Palaeoclimatology, Palaeoecology* 291: 142–153

Tomber, R. and Dore, J. 1998. *The National Roman Fabric Reference Collection. A Handbook* (London: Museum of London Archaeology Service Monograph 2)

Turner, R. 1987. 'Excavations at Apple Tree Close, Pontefract 1987.' *Forum: The Annual Newsletter of CBA Group* 4 1987, 10-11

van der Veen. M. 1989. 'Charred Grain assemblages from Roman-Period Corn Driers in Britain.' *Archaeological Journal* 146, 302-319

Webster, G (ed.). 1976. *Romano-British Coarse Pottery: A Student's Guide. Third Edition* (London: Council for British Archaeology Research Report 6)

Welfare, H. and Swan, V. 1995. *Roman Camps in England.* (London: RCHME)

Wenham, L. and Haywood, B. 1997. *The 1968 to 1970 Excavations in the Vicus at Malton, North*

Yorkshire (Leeds: Yorkshire Archaeological Reports 3)

Whiting, C. 1943 Excavations at Stancil 1938-1939. *Yorkshire Archaeological Journal* 35, 261-9

Williams, D. and Keay, S. 2006. 'Roman Amphorae: a digital resource' http://ads.ahds.ac.uk/catalogue/archive/amphora_ahrb_2005/index.cfm

Willis, S. 2005. *Samian Pottery, a Resource for the Study of Roman Britain and Beyond: the results of the English Heritage funded Samian Project*. An e-monograph. [Supplement to Internet Archaeology 17]: http://intarch.ac.uk/journal/issue17/willis_index.html

Wrathmell, S. 2005. 'Nostell Priory.' *Archaeology and Archives* 21, Autumn 2005, 6

Wrathmell, S. and Nicholson, A. 1990. *Dalton Parlours*. (Leeds: Yorkshire Archaeology 3)

Wight, J. 1972. *Brick Building in England from the Middle Ages to 1550* (London: John Baker Ltd)

Wright, M. 1996. 'The Querns.' In May, J *Dragonby: Report on excavations at an Iron Age/Romano-British settlement in NE Lincolnshire* (Oxford: Oxbow Monographs 61) 365-376

Young, R. and Richardson, J. 2001. 'Parlington Hollins East. The charred plant remains.' In Roberts, I, Burgess, A & Berg, D (eds.) *A New Link to the Past. The Archaeological Landscape of the M1-A1 Link Road*. (Leeds: Yorkshire Archaeology 7) 221-223

Unpublished reports

Beta Analytic 2012. 'Radiocarbon dating results for samples NP09EX021651 and HESEAST2295'. Unpublished report

Bruce, G. 2011. Glass from Nostell Priory. Unpublished report no. OSA09EX02

Chadwick, A. 2009. Research Agenda: The Iron Age and Romano-British Periods in West Yorkshire. West Yorkshire Archaeological Advisory Service

Gaffney, C. 2008. Nostell Priory: Geophysical Survey Report (Report No. 080630/r9125)

Kenward, K. 2012. Nostell Priory Car Park: Report on the investigation of one iron and three copper alloy objects for On-Site Archaeology

York Archaeology Trust Conservation Report No. 2012/13

Leary, R. 2009. Romano-British Pottery from Hemsworth. Unpublished report for ASWYAS

Monteil, G. 2010. Samian ware from a well at Rothwell Haigh. Unpublished report for ASWYAS

Newman, M. 2002. The Designed Landscape of Nostell Priory - A Developmental History. (National Trust Report No. MNNTYR100)

Newman, M. 2006. Nostell Priory Stables and Environs: Archaeological Background and Predictive Model. (National Trust Report No. MNNTYR109)

NAA [Northern Archaeological Associates] 2001. Nostell Priory, West Yorkshire: Archaeological Property Survey

OSA [On-Site Archaeology] 2008a. Nostell Priory. Drainage Replacement Project: Report on an Archaeological Evaluation. (OSA Report No. OSA08EV11)

OSA [On-Site Archaeology] 2008b. Nostell Estate, Land East of Crofton: Desk Based Assessment. (OSA Report No. OSA08DT09)

OSA [On-Site Archaeology] 2008c. The Brewhouse and Refectory, Nostell Estate. Report on an Archaeological Investigation (OSA Report No. OSA08WB04)

OSA [On-Site Archaeology] 2008d. Nostell Car Park. Proposed Visitor Car Park: Report on an Archaeological Evaluation. (OSA Report No. OSA08EV18)

OSA [On-Site Archaeology] 2009. Nostell Priory Car Park: Assessment Report (OSA Report No. OSA09EX02)

OSA [On-Site Archaeology] forthcoming. Nostell Priory Stables Refurbishment: Report on an Archaeological Evaluation and Watching Brief (OSA Report No. OSA10EV03)

Panter, I. 2010. Nostell Priory Car Park: Conservation assessment of small finds for On-Site Archaeology. York Archaeology Trust Conservation Report No. 2010/08

Pinnock, D. 2011. The querns from Nostell Priory. Unpublished report no. OSA09EX02

Simmons, E. 2012. Charred plant remains and charred wood remains from Nostell Priory, Wakefield. (Report no. OSA09EX02)

Tibbles, S. 2011. Ceramic building material from Nostell Priory. Unpublished report no. OSA09EX02

Vyner, B. 2008. Research Agenda: The Neolithic, Bronze Age and Iron Age in West Yorkshire. West Yorkshire Archaeological Advisory Service

WYAS HBRS [West Yorkshire Archaeology Service Historic Building Recording Services] 1996. The 'Monk's Refectory' and the 'Brewhouse', Nostell Priory, West Yorks: An Evaluation of the Standing Buildings

Index